CH00457763

SHAPING EUROPE

Reflections of three MEPs

Lord Plumb
Carole Tongue
and
Florus Wijsenbeek

FEDERAL TRUST

This book is published by the Federal Trust, whose aim is to enlighten public debate on federal issues of national, continental and global government. It does this in the light of its statutes which state that it shall promote 'studies in the principles of international relations, international justice and supranational government.'

The Trust conducts enquiries, promotes seminars and conferences and publishes reports and teaching materials. The Federal Trust is the UK member of the Trans-European Policy Studies Association (TEPSA), a grouping of fifteen think-tanks from member states of the European Union.

Up-to-date information about the Federal Trust can be found on the internet at www.fedtrust.co.uk

© Federal Trust for Education and Research 2000
ISBN 0 901573 99 X

The Federal Trust is a Registered Charity No. 272241
Dean Bradley House, 52 Horseferry Road,
London SW1P 2AF
Company Limited by Guarantee No.1269848

Marketing and Distribution by Kogan Page Ltd
Printed in the European Union

CONTENTS

Florus Wijsenbeek

Introduction

In the history of European integration few steps have been as important as the change from an appointed Assembly to an elected Parliament. More than twenty years ago the first MEPs were elected in direct elections in the summer of 1979 and went to Strasbourg at the beginning of a new experiment in democratic governance on a transnational basis. This was an institutional step change where the United Kingdom took part from the very start.

This volume brings together the reflections of three MEPs who were active in their different ways through their parliamentary activity over the years since then in shaping Europe. They reflect the experience of three different political families in the Parliament – a British Conservative from the European Peoples' Party belonging to the Christian Democratic tradition, a Dutch Liberal and a British Labour member from the Party of European Socialists.

Although they were in the Parliament for many years together and outwardly may have much in common, their viewpoints are very diverse. They write as much from their political as from their personal perspectives.

Lord Plumb views this period magisterially from the position of the only Briton to have been President of the European Parliament. He writes against the background of the Thatcher years, battling against the Prime Minister's and the Conservative Party's growing opposition to all things

European. His commitment to the Parliament and to further European integration ring through his often critical comments on the ever more depressing domestic political scene at the time.

Florus Wijsenbeek writes with unique insight into the early days of the Parliament, since he served as a young man on its staff before he was elected. Then he was in the private office of an earlier President, and his comments on the quality of the institution and the role of MEPs before direct elections could give cause for concern to those who hanker after a return to an appointed Assembly. It was more closely bound to national parties and national parliaments then, but it was clearly still playing in the amateur league. After his election how the view changes, and how Parliament grows in stature and authority. His reflections mix humorous anecdote with a lawyer's shrewd observation of the growing power of Parliament, essentially as a legislator. He does not spare his criticism either for the mixed effects this has had on how parliamentarians approach their work and their new role.

Carole Tongue writes with the same dynamic enthusiasm that she brought to her work as an MEP. You can sense the passion of political argument and the clash of economic interests in her lively description of the battles surrounding the report she wrote on the Directive 'Television without frontiers' and its stormy passage through Parliament. Hers is a story of struggle and success, of honest effort and endeavour, of the never ending demands and delights of a life in European politics.

All three MEPs bear witness to a Parliament that, despite innumerable problems both real and perceived, has now come of age. It is due to the multitudinous efforts of elected MEPs, each in their own idiosyncratic way, each coming with their own traditions, each with their own intellectual and emotional history, but all sharing the desire to be part of a Parliament that represents the people of Europe.

The Treaty of Rome speaks of 'an ever closer union of the peoples of Europe.' The European Parliament has become its clearest political expression yet, and these three MEPs' reflections on the past twenty years, when they were helping to shape Europe, offer the reader telling insights into this continuing process.

Martyn Bond
Director
The Federal Trust
August 2000

Europe - why bother?

Lord Plumb

I always have been a committed European, long before I played an active role in the European Parliament. In 1972, high on my agenda was the negotiation of our entry to the European Economic Community. The Common Agricultural Policy was of course the most important issue we had to face and, as President of the National Farmers Union (NFU), I had to battle with other farm organisations in Europe to get a fair deal. We joined COPA, the Committee of EEC Farmers' Unions, and I became President of that organisation in 1975 for three years, so I was in Brussels on a weekly basis even then.

When I announced my decision to step down from the Presidency of the NFU in January 1979, after ten years in office, and was considering what to do next, several people said to me that I was an obvious candidate for the new direct election to the European Parliament.

Until then, my politics had been 'sectoral,' on behalf of and within the agricultural industry, rather than party based. I had to be independent and deal with parties of all political persuasions and therefore I had never declared a personal party colour during my Presidency of the NFU.

My parents and grandparents were Conservatives and although I had not been an active member, I have always been a supporter and never voted any other way. In my view, only the Conservative Party had the policies capable of achieving the goals I wished to see realised: a sound free-enterprise economy, an emphasis on the responsibilities and liberties of the individual, and an effective and credible defence policy. And was not the Conservative Party 'the party of Europe,' looking back to the post-war vision of Churchill, the travails of Macmillan and the eventual success of Heath? There was no doubt about the Conservative Party's vision of a Britain at last being able to play an enthusiastic and leading role in the development of the EEC; the Thatcherite tragedy lay in the future. I say 'tragedy' advisedly, for I believe that Mrs Thatcher's mistaken attitude to Europe not only led, indirectly, to her own political downfall, which would be sad enough in itself, given her outstanding achievements in other fields, but that its baneful consequences are still with us today, in both Party and country.

Selection and election

In June 1979, I decided to take up the challenge and presented myself as a Conservative candidate in the European elections. It was natural that people should think of me primarily as an agriculturist. This was far from being an advantage in the constituency of the Cotswolds, where I decided to make my bid, for it is not an essentially agricultural region in the way that, for example, parts of Lincolnshire and East Anglia are.

I came through the early rounds of the selection process without incident, but faced stiff competition at the final shortlist. The most gruelling part of the selection procedure, apart from waiting for the final decision, was the ten minutes 'pitch' which each aspiring candidate was invited to make. I decided on a frontal assault. 'Many of you will think of me as a farmers' friend,' I began. I paused for effect and sensed the expectation that I would go on to say 'but ...,' then simply said 'And so I am.' The tension broke at once and I firmly believe that that was the moment which swayed things in my favour. I was delighted to gain the nomination as Conservative candidate.

The election campaign was a strange experience. It was of three weeks duration and the first of its kind, and no party had given much thought as to how to communicate in each constituency with an electorate of approximately half a million. Where did one begin?

A central feature of my campaign was factory visits. One of these in particular stands out in my memory. The manager of an engineering factory in Cheltenham had given my team permission to try our luck at attracting and holding the attention of the workforce during their afternoon tea break in the canteen. A group of card players was identified to me as being the hard-core militant-left shop steward leadership. As I passed their table on the way out, one of then shouted to me 'What y' going to do in this Eurothing for me then?' 'Damn all' I replied. 'Hey,' he said to his mates, 'I might just vote for the geezer, he speaks our language.'

Despite my feeling that I was not really getting to grips with the election or the electorate, the good work done by our loyal party supporters and the reputation the Conservatives enjoyed at that time as the party with sensible policies on Europe, ensured that enough people did vote for this geezer to see me on my way to Strasbourg, Luxembourg and Brussels, the three 'working places' of the European Parliament.

The transition from the NFU to the European Parliament seemed a natural one because of the logical and obvious link with my past experiences and with interests which had been there for decades: Europe, the CAP, world trade and aid to developing countries. I felt motivated and inspired by a new opportunity to contribute to what I believed was the right way to secure prosperity and sustainability in Europe at large, and by the important role I felt Britain could play in the process of further development of European integration. To me, the European Community provided the framework for the only credible 'role' for my country in answer to Dean Acheson's famous dictum about Britain's post-imperial dilemma.

In practical terms, I was not quite sure what to expect. In July, I witnessed the opening of the new European Parliament; the first meeting of the 410 directly elected members and the election of Madame Simone Veil as its first President. I reminded myself of the hopes expressed by Sir Winston Churchill in 1948 (I was 23 at the time) 'when all the little children who are now growing up in this tormented world may find themselves not the victors, nor the vanquished, in the fleeting triumphs of one country over another in the bloody turmoil of destructive war, but the heirs of all treasures of the past and the masters of all the science, the abundance and the glories of the future.'

Many young journalists at the time, however, looked upon the new Parliament as the realisation of a concept that had as its emphasis wartime traumas not relevant to their personal experiences. It was not surprising therefore that the British press did not devote a great deal of serious political coverage to the occasion. Instead, the media concentrated on patriotic fears regarding bureaucratic decision-making and on expressing admiration for the uniquely domestic role which Westminster has enjoyed in our national life over several centuries and the benefits which it has brought. Why bother about the objective of a well functioning European Union for the sake of their generation and the next, when the grounds for the project had not been fully and convincingly explored?

The controversy was evident; many who could vividly remember the Second World War had built-in reservations about all things continental, whilst others, for example Ted Heath, had brought from that experience a determination to see an integrated Europe. Meanwhile, Mrs Thatcher, who had assumed office just three weeks prior to the European elections, was already showing clear signs of developing a blind spot regarding Europe.

Conservative MEPs and Mrs T

During the time I was leader of the British Conservatives in the European Parliament, a responsibility I had for eight years, I had, of course, to transact business with Margaret Thatcher. In point of fact the volume of that business was not all that much, for neither she, nor the party whips, nor Conservative Central Office, ever really got to grips with what the relationship with their own MEPs should be. Those who won seats in 1979 were almost to a man and woman from the earlier pro-European tendency and they had exploited a moment of inattention and indifference in London to mount a significant little coup, in that they elected their own leadership without reference to the Party at home. So the situation was that the sixty-two Conservative MEPs were largely autonomous, financed from the European budget and essentially in favour of further EC integration at the time, whilst the Party at home was now in Government, already eurosceptic in its mood, and not at all in favour even of the existence of the European Parliament - which Mrs Thatcher resolutely continued to call the 'Assembly' for many years to come. There were, of course, frequent contacts between the Party, the Government and us MEPs, especially on specific issues, such as crucial votes in the defence, security and budgetary fields, but there was also an unmistakable distance between us and the Conservative Party at home.

Once or twice a year, usually after the date had been changed umpteen times by Mrs Thatcher's office, the Prime Minister would receive the entire group of British Conservative MEPs at Downing Street. These were always embarrassing encounters. The prevailing atmosphere was one of a meeting between a maiden aunt and a gaggle of rascally nephews, who had clearly been up to mischief on a school trip abroad. On our side, we tried to prepare for these meetings by letting Mrs Thatcher's office know in advance what points we wished to raise, and our policy spokesmen (and women) would put a great deal of effort into preparing working papers for succinct presentation at the meetings. In vain. Apparently, no such preparation was considered necessary on her side and we were frequently subjected instead to a dress rehearsal for a forthcoming speech on a topic which might or might not have any relevance to the European Parliament.

Her responses to the issues we raised were all too obviously off the top of her head. And if she interpreted any comment of ours as being in any way hostile to her point of view, she would invariably preface her reply with the put-down *'Well, in politics, in the real world . . .'* Clearly, as far as she was concerned, we were in neither. I used to wonder 'Why bother?' However, it is some comfort to know from many sources that towards the end she treated her Cabinet in much the same way.

In terms of my personal relations with Mrs Thatcher, I could not complain about the level of civility and courtesy of our exchanges. But regardless of the specific context of our meetings, she would eventually bring the conversation round to agriculture and would invariably preface her questions with flattering remarks how much she valued my expertise in these recondite matters. Firstly, I have the vanity to believe that she did consider I knew a thing or two about the subject, about which she herself had little direct knowledge and suffered from a great deal of contradictory official advice. Secondly, agriculture meant to her the Common Agricultural Policy and therefore 'Europe.' The Common Agricultural Policy was undoubtedly one of the most significant building blocks of the EEC. Britain, however, had played no part in the setting up of the Community, having unwisely declined to join the original six founding member states in their deliberations prior to the drafting of the Treaty of Rome. That treaty had to build a community of interests, with something of major benefit to each of the participants. To put it crudely, as regards the interests of the Franco-German 'locomotive,' the industrial and trade provisions of the treaty can be seen as to the benefit of

Germany, whilst the CAP was very much in the interest of France.

British critics have often alleged that the CAP's main function has been to shore up inefficient French peasant farming at the expense of the consumer and taxpayer. Although such criticisms are partially justified, they are certainly not entirely so, given the higher price of many foodstuffs outside the Community and the benefits to many farmers from the CAP. To Mrs Thatcher, any discussion on the subject was eagerly used to launch her latest anti-Brussels verbal missiles. To me, it was an opportunity to argue, equally eagerly, that the real mistake of that important opening era from a British point of view, had been our absence from the original negotiating table. It is my firm conviction that in the European context, participation with influence is always the best course, whatever the issue may be. To imagine that our non-participation in principle will indefinitely delay our partners, or bring us a long-term advantage is to my mind at best wishful thinking and at worst, folly.

Thirdly, talking agriculture with me spared her the necessity of dialogue on other political issues on which she knew that I and many of my fellow Conservative MEPs did not see eye to eye with her at all.

* * *

I am often asked what was the most important experience for me personally during the twenty years of my mandate as an MEP. It is a very difficult question to answer for many are very much related to personal contacts with individuals; my chairmanship of various groups and committees within the Parliament, as well as experiences at home in my own constituency, and not least the pain and suffering I have witnessed in many countries during my travels.

As I look back, and have to make a choice, there are two experiences which played a major role during that time:

my election as President of the European Parliament in 1987 and as Co-President of the Joint Assembly of the European Union and the African, Caribbean and Pacific (ACP) Countries in 1994.

President of Parliament

The office of President of the European Parliament is often misunderstood. It is frequently compared to that of the Speaker of the House of Commons but the two roles are significantly different. It is true that the most publicly visible aspect of the two roles is more or less the same, namely that of presiding over the plenary session of the House. Even in that regard, the EP President has, in practice, a more complex Chamber to control in that it is multi-national and also contains a much greater variety of party political components. Moreover, national parliaments of long standing have over the decades, or even centuries, evolved not only tried and tested rules of procedure but also firm traditions which provide precedents for the orderly management of business in the House. The youthful European Parliament, on the other hand, whilst it had an initial set of rules of procedure, was obliged to find its way and to achieve within a few years a level of maturity to which the national parliaments had taken a long period of time to evolve.

The President of the European Parliament, in addition to his role as presiding officer (which he delegates for many debates to one of the fourteen Vice-Presidents) also chairs the meetings of the Bureau and the Conference of Group Chairmen, thus taking responsibility for guiding the decision-making process for much of Parliament's work. Since the European Parliament has no 'Government' within its ranks in the manner of a national Parliament, it falls to the President to lead the institutional representations of the Parliament towards the other European institutions and also to the outside world. Some of this work is largely ceremonial, but it also frequently involves political initiative and reaction, which means that the President must often walk a tightrope between his own instincts and the likely positions (where these are not already established through adopted resolutions or other decisions) of the House as a whole.

A further difficulty is that, as part of the checks and balances, the President is usually politically in a minority, in terms of the right-left divide, within the Bureau, since that balance is normally a fine one and since the office of President counts as two vice-presidential posts in the overall weightings. Thus a President from the centre-right usually chairs a Bureau with an overall left-of-centre majority, and visa versa. The post of President is therefore not one of intrinsic power, but one of considerable responsibility and, if used wisely, of influence.

It was just after the 1984 European Elections, when Egon Klepsch, Chairman of the EPP (European People's Party), came to see me. At that time, the number of British Conservative members was considerably reduced. The new Parliament was balanced between left and right, and the mathematics of the situation dictated that the EPP could only win if they had all our EDG (European Democratic Group) votes. We extracted a written assurance from Egon Klepsch that in 1987 the EPP would support an EDG candidate.

Not until late 1986 did I ever contemplate the possibility of my becoming a Presidential candidate. When it happened, it was totally unexpected. In fact, I was more or less forced to enter the competition in a great hurry when shortly before the Christmas break a small group of colleagues from the EPP and my own group put it to me bluntly that with my candidature, the European Democratic Group had a sporting chance, but only a sporting chance of winning the Presidency; with any other candidate we were certain to lose. This calculation was based not only on sentiment within the EPP, but also on the likely willingness of members of the other centre-right groups, namely the Liberals and the RDE (the Gaullists and Fianne Fáil) to vote for a British Tory.

So I said yes to the invitation to run, then swiftly set about campaigning as best I could in the short time available to me. I knew that one of the other candidates would be Marco Panella, the brilliant but erratic leader of the Italian Radical Party. His votes, once he fell out of the race as he surely would, would be crucial for the surviving 'big two' candidates, who would be the Spanish Socialist Enrique Baron Crespo and myself. Baron had a head start, being sure of the support of the largest group, plus the Communists. My only chance was to hold on to as many as possible of the centre-right votes and to challenge him for a share of the smaller groups' support and that of the non-attached members. I had a difficult meeting with the Liberal Group, some of whose members pressed me hard on what I could offer them in return for their support. I felt that my reply, which went no further than a commitment to be as effective a President as possible was not much of an 'offer,' but the leader of the Portuguese delegation surprised me, and probably saved the day, by saying half in jest that he would vote for me because he could believe my lack of promises!

The most delicate operation of all was my meeting with Jean-Marie Le Pen, Leader of the French National Front, many of whose policy statements and attitudes, especially as regards race relations, were anathema to democrats of both left and right. Indeed it was rumoured that moves were afoot to isolate his group within the Parliament to the utmost degree, amounting to the ostracism of its members in the daily life and work of the institution. I was warned by one of his members, Jean Olivier d'Ormesson, who had defected to the National Front on being dropped from the candidates' list in 1984, that Le Pen privately blamed the centre right for hatching this plot, and that his group were likely to vote in bloc for Enrique Baron as a result.

It may seem strange, to British eyes, that the extreme right would prefer the left to the centre right, but that has often been a feature of the French political landscape over the past thirty years. I knew that if Le Pen did throw his votes behind my rival, I had no chance of winning. I asked to see Le Pen, who insisted that the meeting take place in his office in the Palais Bourbon, seat of the National Assembly. Jean Oliver d'Ormesson acted as broker and I travelled to Paris accompanied only by Robert Ramsay, our Group Secretary General. It was an awkward mission. News of the meeting could easily have leaked out. I was at Le Pen's mercy as regards its confidentiality and could in any case have been spotted in the precincts of the Assembly (I drew the line at false whiskers or dark glasses). Such news would almost certainly have driven away enough of my natural supporters to have sunk my boat; but it was the last throw of the dice.

Le Pen was uncharacteristically reserved and downbeat and appeared to treat the meeting as a casual exchange of views about how Parliament was organised. My only theme was that, if elected, I would treat all groups according to the spirit and the letter of the rules. It was in fact my conviction, since strengthened by experience, that such an approval is the only sensible one for a President to employ; I have seen others get into a deep mire by trying to favour, or do down, a particular group by the misuse of their position. I have no idea what impressions Le Pen took away from the meeting - d'Ormesson volunteered no assessment afterwards - but news of it did not leak out and the final electoral arithmetic would certainly suggest that the National Front MEPs either voted for me or abstained.

Some of my supporters expressed the view that the Irish Fianne Fáil members were unlikely to bring themselves to vote for a British Tory. I did not share that pessimism as I had had extremely good relations with many of them, even before my EP days, based on a shared interest in matters of agriculture.

The day of the Presidential election, 20th February 1987 was a long and hectic one. All the other such elections, both before and since, have, on the day, been devoid of real drama. This has either been because the two biggest groups, the EPP and the Socialists, who between them can nearly always muster an overall majority, have made a pact that one will provide a candidate for the first half of the legislative period and support the other's candidate for the second half, or, as in 1999, because the candidate of one group has had so many 'neutral' votes to begin with as to be a racing certainty. In principle I am in favour of a genuine, open race, but I can't recommend it as being good for one's nerves.

It was a nail-biting finish with 241 votes for me against 236 for Baron Crespo. It left me emotionally drained, but after a brief celebration with my closest advisers, I was pitched the next morning straight into chairing the meeting of the new Bureau. This marked the start of an intense thirty month period of activity during which practically every minute of each day was programmed around my duties as President.

Support and innovation

My first and most urgent task was to select my personal staff, known in Euro jargon by its French title of the 'Cabinet.' This consisted of six administrators and fourteen support staff, drawn from two-thirds of the member states represented in Parliament, thus providing a good spread of linguistic capabilities and national cultural awareness. The smooth and efficient functioning of the Cabinet is essential to the success of any presidency, since it not only gives the President the personal support and organisational framework he or she needs in order to operate day by day, but also provides the services of Parliament with detailed guidance for their activities. The general 'feel' of the overall administration of the institution is determined, to a large extent, by the success or otherwise of the Cabinet under its President.

Several Presidents have brought in administrators from their national civil service, often with no direct experience of the workings of the European Parliament, to occupy the most senior posts in their cabinet. The principal advantages of such a decision are to give the President a privileged link to his home capital, and to mark his own independence from the General Secretariat of Parliament. However, I have always considered these advantages to be overrated in practice and to be far outweighed by the disadvantage of having the most senior members of the team floundering around, in unfamiliar and sometimes shark infested water for the best part of a year while they learned how the European Parliament worked. I believe, therefore, that I made the right choice in seeking to combine outside independence with insider experience.

I persuaded Robert Ramsay to come with me from the European Democratic Group as my Director of the Cabinet. For his number two I obtained Emyr Jones Parry, who had worked for the Foreign and Commonwealth Office as Counsellor in the UK Permanent Representation in Brussels, with special responsibility for liaison with the European Parliament. They and the rest of the team worked hard and harmoniously together for the next two and a half years. Staff problems, the bane of quite a few Presidencies I have known, never took up a minute of my time and the atmosphere of a united family team was predominant.

The primordial duty of the President is, of course, to preside and whilst I had had long years of experience in chairmanship at various levels, including European institutional bodies, chairing the plenary sessions of Parliament and the Bureau was certainly new territory. The former duty was naturally the riskier of the two, since it took place in public, with totally free access given to the news media, including constant TV recording of proceedings. However, in some ways I came to enjoy it more, with the exception of the complex voting sessions on important issues, such as the passage of the budget. These could go on for hours and were at times mind-numbingly boring, yet total concentration was demanded at all times, since any slip-up, for example, incorrectly putting to the House a complicated split vote on a crucial amendment, could cause enormous confusion, especially through interpretation, and take ages to unravel. In a comparatively young institution such as the European Parliament, the President and his Table staff do not have at their disposal the benefit of the distilled procedural wisdom of the centuries, such as Erskine May in Westminster, to guide their rulings on points of order or other procedural conundrums.

So there is always an element of adventurous improvisation on the part of the President and his administrative supporters who sit alongside him on the 'perch' whenever his intervention is called for in a difficult situation. The Secretary General of the Parliament, the immensely gifted Sicilian, Enrico Vinci, was a genius at the creative use of the Rules of Procedure. One of my predecessors in office, the Dutchman Piet Dankert, once complained about the nightmare of having suddenly to give off the cuff legal interpretations to be applied to parliamentary business. 'But,' commented a colleague, 'surely it was a comfort to have Vinci at your elbow?' 'Not really,' replied Dankert. 'You see, as a Calvinistic Dutchman, I wanted to know the appropriate rule before giving my answer, but when I turned to Vinci for advice, he would whisper 'Tell me the answer you want, Mr President, and I will find you a rule.' And indeed, he could.

One of the innovations which I surreptitiously introduced on an informal basis was at the start of business on the Monday afternoon of each plenary part-session in Strasbourg. Members spent the morning and part of the afternoon travelling and started late in the day by having group meetings to put the finishing touches to their political tactics for the week ahead. Then at five o'clock sharp the plenary begins, with a high level of attendance, as the first item of business is to finalise the arrangements for the business of the House for the next five days. This set piece concentrates the political mind quite sharply, for there is much inter-group manoeuvring, aimed at switching the debate slots for various reasons, to obtain some advantage, for example, in terms of likely media coverage, or to stymie one's opponents' procedural tricks. In short, the stuff of all democratic parliamentarians' rough and tumble. I had noticed that some skilful operators occasionally used this point on the agenda, under the guise of a question to the President or through some spurious linkage with a report down on the Draft Agenda for debate that week, to raise matters of public interest or concern.

My predecessors had all exercised a strict control on such non-pre-packaged interventions and cut the initiators off at an early stage of their speeches, with the quite correct ruling that the matter being raised was not apposite to the fixing of the Draft Agenda. I decided to be more lenient in the matter, and to let this unscheduled mini-debate on topical issues run for a little while each Strasbourg Monday, so this slot in the programme came to be known as 'Henry's Happy Half Hour.' It was not at all popular with the movers and shakers of the House, who looked on this interlude it created as a diversion.

One irrefutable formal objection to my leniency was that every Thursday morning in Strasbourg, there was an 'Urgent and Topical Debate' for three hours, so there should have been no need for the informal opening debate which I allowed to creep into the habits of the House. However, I found the Thursday debate most unsatisfactory as a parliamentary occasion, in that the real political action surrounding these sessions happened off-stage in the group offices. There the motions for debate were drafted and attempts made between group representatives to hammer out compromises as regards joint texts. Group Chairmen, meeting in private early in the week would select five or six topics for debate, of which two were regular features, namely human rights issues and natural disasters. The latter, which were often cynically referred to as 'the bad weather' items, sometimes had a very practical significance. For example, if it related to damage to property or crops in a Community region, a sympathetic resolution adopted by Parliament would greatly increase the chances of European monies being made available in compensation to the region concerned.

In order to accommodate as many draft resolutions as possible one of the tricks of the trade was to combine in a single resolution references to several, often only spuriously related, matters, which did nothing to enhance the overall coherence of the operation. Once all this wheeling and dealing had been completed behind the scenes, political interest in the debate itself waned. Moreover, by Thursday many MEPs were engaged in activities outside the Chamber, for example looking after visitors' groups or attending sectoral meetings in their particular field of interest. So, apart from those waiting their turn to speak, the House tended to be sparsely populated, with only the occasional lively and well-attended debate.

By contrast, during 'Henry's Happy Half Hour,' there was almost always genuine controversy, a full House and spontaneous expressions of opinions from the elected representatives of the peoples of Europe about the burning issues of the day. Sadly, the tendency since has been to swing back to controlled orthodoxy in this matter. I believe that the problem of allowing proper expression to 'the voice of the people' has yet to be satisfactorily resolved.

Backbenchers and the bureau

It must be said that in all modern parliaments, it is difficult to provide for a worthwhile contribution to debate from the backbenchers, who are, after all, the direct representatives of grass roots public opinion. The pressure on parliamentary time, largely due to the need to bring forward ever weightier programmes of legislation, means that the individual member is forced more and more into the role of lobby fodder for his party and all too seldom succeeds in speaking his mind from the floor of the House. The problem is all the more acute in the European Parliament, since the number of plenary days each month varies between only four and six full days.

As regards the allocation of speaking time, the European Parliament is at least fair: the total debating time available is divided in advance amongst the groups using our old favourite, the d'Hondt proportional system; then within each group there is a further share out, according to the respective responsibilities in the field concerned, or the particular interests of national delegations. It is within each group that the hardest horse-trading is done and the result is usually to break the group's allocation into increasingly small units in order to meet, however frugally, the many demands for speaking time. The final details of this share out are notified in advance to the President who has the job of keeping each speaker on schedule, the duration of each intervention being shown by means of a large digital stop watch ticking away the seconds on the wall.

I sometimes had the feeling that I was impersonating a TV game-show host when I gave the floor to a member with the ritual words 'Mr Brown, for one minute,' – perhaps on a topic such as – 'on peace in the Middle East.' Such sound-bite opportunities are often ludicrous in the context of the overall debate, but they do have the merit of permitting a large number of speakers to take part - certainly far more than in most national parliaments. The technical infrastructure of the European Parliament gives the President an all-powerful disciplinary weapon: if a Member disregards a warning from the 'perch' that he is approaching the end of his time allocation, the President has only to press a 'disconnect' button on the desk in front of him to leave the speaker without amplification and worse, interpretation, so that he is just a voice crying in the wilderness.

Seasoned parliamentarians frequently find ways round the rules and agreed speaking times to achieve extra attention for their point of view. In the European Parliament, one much used loophole at that time was the 'Explanation of Vote' clause of the Rules of Procedure. Invoking this right, a member could, in explaining his vote, put over the guts of the speech he would have liked to make in the debate. Admittedly this *post facto* intervention could no longer, by definition, affect the vote; but it allowed the Member to place his views on record, and to publicise them to his home media as having been delivered in the European Parliament. Nowadays Parliamentarians are strongly encouraged to submit their explanations of votes in writing, in the same way that opinions are frequently written into the record of the US Congress.

Another ruse I had to deal with was the 'Point of Order.' Members who rise in their place with their arms aloft and hands crossed can, in principle, expect to catch the President's eye and be allowed to raise a point of order. Sometimes this was genuine and required a procedural ruling from the President. In the case of important and complex issues, there was available the fall back position of referring the matter to the Parliamentary Committee responsible, *inter alia*, for Rules. But more often than not the 'Point of Order' was little more than a mini political speech, cleverly advanced under the camouflage of a procedural argument. Invariably in such cases, when I intervened to rule the alleged point of order 'inadmissible,' the culprit would adopt a posture of outraged innocence of the kind common among penalised football players who have just scythed the feet from under the opposing striker and been caught by the ref.

On the whole I tried to be as liberal as possible and, above all, to ensure that the smaller groups got a fair crack of the whip, in the overall interests of democracy. My fundamental belief in the need for a strong parliamentary institution at the heart of the European enterprise is coupled with my conviction that the European Parliament should come across to ordinary citizens as something comprehensible and worthwhile which acts on their behalf. Certain practical problems, shared by all national parliaments, got in the way of that ideal, some of which even had their origin in technological advances. I cite just two examples. The fact that members can follow proceedings in the Chamber on TV sets in their offices whilst getting on with other aspects of their parliamentary business, means that frequently during plenary sessions the MEPs actually in the House are vastly outnumbered by the visitors in the gallery, who are understandably disappointed by the deserted scene below them. Secondly, electronic voting by smart card obviously makes voting much easier - but automatically increases the temptation to vote too often. There is a fine balance to be struck between taking occasional decisions on important matters of general principle and voting on every possible legislative detail, on the premise, of course that 'the devil is in the detail.' In my view, the European Parliament still tilts too much towards the latter course and in my days of presiding over several hours of voting at a stretch I probably held that view even more strongly than today.

Voting sessions apart I quickly came to enjoy the challenges of presiding at plenary session. I hope that I was able in some measure to lighten the tone of the formal proceedings and develop a more human rapport between the President on his perch and the individual member on the floor of the House.

Presiding over the EP-Bureau was a different kind of experience, though equally challenging. The Bureau, made up of the Vice-Presidents, met on average twice monthly and was joined in a third meeting by the eight political group chairmen, to form what was known at Assembly as the 'Enlarged Bureau.' This always struck me as an unfortunate nomenclature, with overtones of an unpleasant medical condition; occasionally it felt like one, too, especially whenever there were clashes between group chairmen, who joined the Bureau on these occasions, and Vice-Presidents of the same group, each believing himself to be senior to the other in the political pecking order. In reality there could be little doubt that the chairmen of the largest three or four groups had more 'clout' than most Vice-Presidents, but the problem was that there was no clear power structure, no obvious hierarchy, nor indeed clear guidelines as to who should do what.

There were separate competences for the Bureau and Enlarged Bureau written into an annex of the Rules of Procedure, which largely reserved the more 'political' decisions for the larger entity. But in practice there were many grey areas and if a Vice-President or a number of Vice-Presidents did not like the way a particular discussion was developing in the Bureau, one method to delay the decision was to contrive to have the matter referred to the Enlarged Bureau. After my Presidency, the group chairmen succeeded in having a Conference of Group Presidents established as a separate entity to the Bureau. Even with a new set of guidelines, however, the issue of respective competence has not yet been entirely resolved, though my impression in recent years has been that the balance of power and influence has shifted towards the group chairmen and away from the Vice-Presidents.

As the person responsible for chairing both the Bureau and the Enlarged Bureau I was often caught in the middle of these turf wars; fortunately I became accepted as the honest broker, the fact that I came from a group other than the two giants helped in this respect. Despite the need for interpretation facilities, the meetings of both entities were quite intimate and detailed, the work being carried out on the basis of high quality position and option papers prepared by the services of the General Secretariat.

The role of Chairman demanded great patience, as most issues had to have at least one *tour de table* to give everyone their say; and also great concentration, in order to be able to spot the most potentially fruitful line for achieving consensus. Decisions arrived at without a vote always had the best chance of being successful in practice, but there were inevitably issues which had to be put to the vote. Within the Bureau, voting was more straightforward in the sense that the Vice-Presidents numerically reflected the strength of the political forces in the House; amongst the group chairmen, however, the forces represented by the leaders of the largest two groups could each be six or seven times greater than those represented by the leaders of the two smallest groups. There was no weighted voting system, but if a decision looked as though it was going to be distorted because of this factor, we had the fall-back position of referring the matter to the full House. That tended, however, to be very much a last resort, as the group leaders were wary of putting the fate of important decisions into the hands of the backbenchers who, as they would have said, might not have had the opportunity to acquaint themselves with all the issues fully.

It was fascinating to observe the differing debating and negotiating styles of the various nationalities. It seemed to me that in this regard there is a basic 'North-South' cultural divide, the South being represented by the countries of Latin cultural origins, the North by the rest. France, though linguistically in the Southern category, represents, as befits a country stretching from the Straits of Dover to the Mediterranean, a half-way house between the two. The French believe this to be an important national advantage, but the downside is that they are frequently mistrusted by both camps, however much they are admired for their powers of analysis.

The Northern and Southern European styles differ profoundly from one another; both have their advantages and disadvantages. The Northern approach is as simple and direct as possible, is more quickly understood and takes much less time to put across; the Southern approach is more elliptical and subtle and takes a great deal of time to convey. Indeed, whilst everyone pays lip service to the virtues of brevity, I have the feeling that Southern Europeans, perhaps sub-consciously, equate brevity of presentation with weakness of argument. The biggest plus for the Northern style is clarity and speed. The Latins, however, can often find solutions where others have failed, through their genius for widening the angle through which a particular problem is viewed, in this way identifying acceptable compromises as part of a package which goes well beyond the original discussion. As a Northerner, I had to train myself to listen very attentively to interventions by Southerners, in order to be aware of messages being conveyed between the lines, either in the sense of polite rejection of ideas already advanced, or of possible openings for eventual agreement beyond the speaker's first adopted position. I did not attempt, however, to modify my own style of chairmanship from that which I evolved during my days as leader of the National Farmers' Union and Chairman of COPA and the European Democratic Group. This was because I believe that whilst within Europe it is important to understand and appreciate the distinctive cultural traditions and heritage of our various backgrounds, this very diversity is one of our greatest riches and we should not even make attempts at homogenisation.

Constraints and change

Once the initial flurry of activity following my election as President was over, I set about the task of deciding upon a number of goals and of attempting to organise my life in a way which would give me the best chance of attaining them, at least in some measure. Rigorous time management, set against clear objectives, was absolutely essential, since there are so many external demands made on the President's time and so many tempting invitations to visit interesting places, that without a game plan of one's own one would undoubtedly be carried hither and thither at the mercy of umpteen winds and currents. All days were obviously going to be long and hard, but fortunately my established office habits - based on my experience from boyhood of rising early to milk cows and, if necessary, staying in the fields by moonlight to bring in the harvest - stood me in good stead.

The problem of operating from three working places was inevitably a complicating factor. Unlike most MEPs, I now had to visit Luxembourg quite regularly, as I was formally in charge of the activities of the General Secretariat. The journey by road from Brussels takes only two hours, mostly through the pleasant landscape of the Ardennes, but it was the disruption to the timetable of my Private Office which was the real penalty.

My relations with the trade unions and the Staff Committee were on the whole cordial. This was mainly because I supported one of their fundamental tenets, namely their insistence on the maintenance and development of an independent European Civil Service with a truly European ethos drawn from the treaties, as opposed to an *ad hoc* administrative corps with some degree of national tutelage. I think they also appreciated my willingness to look at the practical difficulties of their jobs: I recall being particularly warmly received in the middle of the night when I made an unannounced visit to the print shop, where the documents for the next day's parliamentary business were rolling off the presses. Even a task such as producing the verbatim report of the preceeding day's plenary session, the European Parliament's equivalent of Hansard, requires a much greater effort of co-ordination and management control, because of the need to cover the working languages: nine in those days, now increased to eleven.

To the disappointment of some of my friends, I had foresworn as a presidential candidate my right to campaign in favour of a single seat for the European Parliament. I had done so not for calculated electoral purposes - there were as many votes to be lost as to be won on such an issue - but because I believed that it was inappropriate for the President of the Parliament to campaign on an issue on which there were deep divisions within his own institution. It is one thing for the President to throw his personal weight behind a campaign if the matter has been the subject of debate, followed by a resolution adopted by an overwhelming majority in the House; it is quite another matter if the issue is one which is both sensitive and divisive. Nor could I ever accept on this or any other matter, that the President could retain a total freedom of expression by making a distinction each time between his own personal standpoint and the official institutional line. To have tried to do so would have led to confusion, and would have weakened the representative authority of the President's office.

Having reviewed my responsibilities and assessed the opportunities available to me within the constraints imposed by time and the limits of my office, I decided on a limited number of objectives for the presidency. The first priority had to be the successful application of the Single European Act, then awaiting final ratification and its coming into force as it affected Parliament. Linked to that goal was my ambition to improve the standing of the European Parliament in the overall set of institutional inter-relationships. That would, in its turn, serve my third purpose, namely the raising of the Parliament's profile both within the member states, especially the UK, and in the outside world.

I have always believed that success in leadership depends largely on keeping one's aims to the minimum number of essentials, and on harnessing the energy of one's forces to the tasks necessary for the achievement of those aims. In retrospect, I can see that only my first priority was fully met; the others depended on that success but there was not time to see them entirely achieved during my term of office. Nevertheless, a start was made and the improvement of the European Parliament's profile and standing in public opinion is an on-going task, by no means nearing its end at the time of writing.

The successful implementation of the Single European Act, (and from my point of view particularly the new role of the European Parliament for which it provides) is undoubtedly the most important European advance of the 1980s. In laying down the framework which enabled the creation of the single market over the period up to the end of 1992, the SEA, once applied, ensured that the old 'Common Market' progressed so far along the road to a single economy that there could be no turning back. As a Conservative, I was delighted that the sort of single market to be achieved was - in its insistence on genuinely free competition and a market liberated from the former distortions such as national restrictive practices, what were usually disguised behind such labels as 'precautionary health measures' - essentially one in tune with my party's economic philosophy. There would be irritations later on, over such left-inspired items as the Social Chapter, but fundamentally there has never been any doubt that the single European market is rooted firmly in the concept of free market economic principles.

As regards the European Parliament, the Single European Act introduced a new legislative procedure for a broad category of laws, which I felt had the potential to enable the institution to progress to another stage of development. Of course, this advance was a far cry from the role envisaged for the European Parliament in Spinelli's Draft Treaty of Union. Nonetheless, it was significant. Over the range of legislation necessary to complete the single market and some new areas of Community policy, in particular research, laws at European level would no longer be subject to the existing consultation procedure, involving one reading in the Parliament. In future they would attract a new 'cooperation' procedure, under which the European Parliament's opinion and textual amendments would be passed to the Council, via the Commission. Parliament would then be re-consulted, on the basis of new proposals, which would be the subject of renewed consideration in Committee and a new opinion, including textual amendments, determined by means of a second reading.

As unanimity in the Council, historically, had been relatively difficult to achieve, this last provision gave the European Parliament's texts a vastly superior value, measured against their influence in the original consultative procedure (which continued to be applied to legislation in categories not covered by cooperation). And of course the very existence of Parliament's new powers meant that the other two institutions were *nolens volens* obliged to take us more seriously at every stage and to try from the outset to present us with proposals which had, in the light of known priorities a reasonable chance of being broadly acceptable. This increase in the Parliament's influence was also extended, by similar procedure, to the adoption of agreements between the Community and outside countries and to agreement on future enlargements.

I was convinced that the performance of the European Parliament in the early days of the new dispensation would be crucial to the reputation and future development of the institution. Were we to fail the test, either through a lack of organisation or through irresponsible action or a low quality of work, our chance of becoming a serious player in the legislative business of Europe would vanish, if not forever, then certainly for a very long time. There were many in national capitals who had never wanted to see a directly elected European Parliament and who would have been more than happy for it to be curtailed indefinitely as a 'talking shop,' which would undoubtedly have been its destiny had it not cleared the hurdle of applying the Single European Act.

There were three aspects to the challenge: to coordinate the work of the Parliamentary Committees in such a way that they were geared up to operating a systematic legislative programme to a tight timetable (Parliament's formal reaction to proposals was in the new scheme of things normally required within three months); to organise the necessary administrative support for such action, in particular through the setting up of inter-institutional working groups to establish and monitor the critical path of each piece of draft legislation; and, most difficult of all, to change the whole ethos of the European Parliament at both political and administrative levels, into that of a serious legislative assembly.

That was a tall order and time was short. Things could have been worse on the timing front, as the Single European Act had been expected to come into effect in January 1987, coinciding almost exactly with the start of my Presidency. Providentially, there had been a delay in the ratification process, which provided a valuable breathing space from my point of view, meaning that the Single European Act did not come into force until 1st July 1987.

The necessary changes were not easy to bring about, but they were accomplished, and in good time. Until then, the European Parliament had certainly undertaken a measure of routine legislative activity in partnership with the Commission and Council, but had not been an essentially legislative House. As an institution we had managed though to make an impact on certain policies in a non-legislative way. For example, within the work of my own group, I think of the influence exerted on European thinking by the 'Freedom of the Skies' campaign waged by Lord Bethell against the airline cartels and their price-fixing activities; or of the brilliant animal welfare public relations exercise mounted by Stanley Patrick Johnson against the practice of culling seals in Canada. But such sporadic successes would not, in the longer term, constitute a viable *raison d'être* for a European institution. Such 'own initiatives' would inevitably become rarer in the future, under the increased pressure of the Parliamentary and the legislative timetable.

The growing up process involved a change in the status of the Committee Chairmen. They now had to programme the agendas of their meetings to ensure that legislative work had priority and that it was seriously organised, both as regards timing and technical content. This had the political side effect of enhancing the status of the position adopted. Similarly, the need for monthly co-ordination of legislative work between Committee Chairmen brought increased importance to that body, which was to develop as a new power centre within the House, at times rivalling the Bureau and the Enlarged Bureau.

The changes had implications for inter-group relations, too. Whilst generally I am in favour of the various political families setting out their stalls and carrying on their business in total transparency, I am nevertheless grateful, in the institutional interests of the European Parliament, that, particularly in the early days of the application of the Single European Act, there was a fair amount of abnormal consultation and covert cooperation between the two main groups. That cooperation was facilitated by the fact that the two main group leaders, Rudi Arndt (Socialist) and Egon Klepsch (EPP) were willing, when necessary, to work together. They were known as 'the two Big Germans,' a nickname which had several layers of meaning: they were certainly big physically (knuckles of pork, sauerkraut and beer leaving their mark); they were big in terms of their political 'hitting' power both within their respective groups and within Parliament; and they proved to be big in that they had the vision to realise that the success of Parliament's role vis-à-vis the Single European Act depended to a significant degree on *ad hoc* understandings between them.

Changes caused by the Single European Act also had immediate and longer-term effects on the backbench membership of the Parliament, particularly as regards attendance and the seriousness with which Parliamentary duties were performed. I am not being in the least chauvinistic when I record that British MEPs, regardless of party, had by and large always carried out their duties in a conscientious way. Those who held dual mandates, being Westminster MPs as well, were particularly industrious - though it gradually came to be accepted that the burden of the dual mandate was too great for any individual and the practice has since died out. The same could not be said for some other nationalities, the French and Italians being the worst offenders. Although things have changed radically in both countries since, for example through legal limitations on the number of public offices a citizen can occupy simultaneously, at that time both attendance rates and the work rate of quite a large number of members made a major contribution to the caricature of the lazy, junketing, snout-in-the-trough MEP. Such caricatures are much more swiftly created than dismantled and even today, hard working MEPs suffer from the lingering negative aspects of the image transmitted in the early days of the European Parliament.

In reality, the profound change came in 1987, when groups had to insist on proper attendance, serious work and serious voting, on pain of various sanctions. Political group meetings, which hitherto had often been held in one of the twelve national capitals, were now largely concentrated, for the sake of convenience, in Brussels, thus adding to that city's role as the *de facto* centre of Community operations.

Presidents and politicians

Of the three Institutions with their own Presidents, Jacques Delors led the Commission throughout my time but there were nine national ministers in the Council in rota. The more I saw of Delors the more I liked him. His cerebral powers were respected and admired by all, even though his professional style of delivery could be off-putting. Sometimes in a meeting he would be asked a question which appeared to require a one sentence answer. Before replying he would pause for several seconds, as though he did not know the answer. Then he would begin, in a totally matter-of-fact way with 'I think there are six aspects to this,' and proceed to deliver himself of a perfectly constructed, coherent, multi-faceted analysis, which could have been printed verbatim and without correction in the next day's *Le Monde Diplomatique*. But he was not all macroeconomic forecasts and inter-institutional relationships; he found equal stimulus in jazz, football or the tour de France, and on big occasions would interrupt meetings in his office for clandestine TV viewings at which he would display all the guilty delight of a truant schoolboy. What I particularly liked about him was his readiness to admit that he did not know things about a particular subject. For example, I recall his asking a German minister about details of the background to the setting up of the Federal Republic in 1948; he did so without any embarrassment at this perhaps surprising gap in his knowledge and yet displaying a modesty with which few French intellectuals are blessed.

Looking further ahead, it has remained a mystery to many why Delors did not, at the last minute, run for the Presidency of France against Jacques Chirac in 1995. I believe that in the last analysis the crucial difference between these two highly gifted and ambitious men was that Chirac's political appetite for power was the keener. A fear of failure in such a tight situation must have been common to both. In Chirac's case his appetite was stronger than his fear; with Delors it was the reverse.

As regards the national ministers I met, both during the Council Presidency held by their particular member state and in other contexts, I was struck above all by how few of them were fully tuned in to the European theme of which their own activities were part. British Foreign Office Ministers were notable exceptions to this pattern, though I had the impression that in London they felt constrained to hide their light under a bushel, as 'Europeans' were never going to be flavour of the month.

One of the standard duties of the President of the European Parliament is to make, within a few months of taking office, an official visit to each of the capitals of the member states. Typically such a visit will include an audience with the head of state, a courtesy call on the Speaker of the national parliament, and meetings with ministers who have departmental interests closely involved with European Community affairs, as well as with opposition party leaders and leaders of organisations such as employers and trade unions. Although the overall content of each such visit was very similar, true to the theme of European diversity, each had its own particular flavour.

Looking back, the distinctive characteristic was already established from the moment the presidential limousine set off from the end of the red carpet at the airport with its accompanying escort of motorcycle outriders. In Bonn, for example, the car was preceded by a V-shaped formation of ten outriders who moved at moderate speed but with the utmost grace and within centimetres of one another. One had the impression of watching a display of precision riding at a military tattoo. In Rome, on the other hand, one had at that point of the visit the impression that one was not only a spectator at, but also a participant in a cross between a bank raid get-away and a 500cc TT race, as the motorcade and motorbikes roared through the traffic at breakneck speed, outriders dashing ahead to secure a clear passage, and forcing vehicles coming from the sides to screech to the left. Restful it was not, but symptomatic.

On the second day of the official visit to Italy, my party arrived at the office of the Prime Minister, only to find that no one was expecting us. After a ten minutes' wait, feverish telephoning and a security frisking, I was finally shown in to see the Head of Government, Bettino Craxi. He had just received a severe mauling in the *Camera dei Deputati* and at that moment was the glummest politician I had ever met. Perhaps the problems which were later to take him into exile in Tunisia as a fugitive from justice were already casting their shadow. Usually Italian politicians are extremely upbeat about Europe - cynics used to say that was because they welcomed the prospect of a supranational rescue from the chaos of their national politics - but not even that topic could shake Craxi from his gloom. When he saw how the political parties and the press behaved, he confided, he simply despaired of democracy.

Fortunately, this was not a mood widespread amongst my other Italian hosts. A courtesy call on the Pope was arranged as an annex to this official visit to Italy. Protocol was, as I had expected, superficially complicated. On the arrival of my party in the Vatican itself the stiffness continued. The system for the reception of VIP visitors granted a private audience with the Pope involved passing the visitor through a series of antechambers, in each of which a few minutes were spent talking to an ever more senior clerical official who then scurried away, presumably to update the briefing notes for the Pope on what points were likely to arise outside the agreed agenda. All this struck me as a trifle excessive for a courtesy call, but was no doubt standard procedure. However, when the personal study of the Pope was finally reached, the bureaucratic trappings fell away and my audience with John Paul II was extremely relaxed and ranged far and wide, well beyond the pre-arranged parameters of the discussion.

The Pope's main 'official' interest was in the relationship between the European Community institutions and the Council of Europe and how the two could best jointly affect developments in the Soviet Union and its satellites. I was surprised at the vagueness of his knowledge about the constitutional differences between the two European entities - he apparently had not fully taken on the degree to which the EC's legislative and policy action had already been integrated. But his deep knowledge of central and eastern Europe shone through in his insights into what was fermenting there. Even he, however, whilst optimistic that in the long run Communism could not hold sway over so many people who in their hearts rejected it, did not foresee how swiftly and fundamentally things were to change throughout the Soviet bloc. I asked him whether he thought that Gorbachov's reform would successfully continue. He paid tribute to what the Soviet leader was trying to achieve within the existing system, but expressed, sadly, his opinion that these efforts would end in failure and in the short term at least, be reversed. 'His own associates will simply not allow him to go on down the path of reform', he said. I asked him whether that was the opinion of a Pole or a Pope. He smiled at the impertinence of my question, then reflected long and hard before replying 'probably both.'

After the exchange of official gifts, the Pope prolonged the meeting for another fifteen minutes, to receive my staff and to talk more generally about his concerns for Western Europe. He was particularly exercised about the lack of idealism amongst young people in general and the failure of all the churches to engage their attention. 'Europe' as a concept would have to offer more than the prospect of material improvement and the churches would have to strive harder to communicate with the young if a spiritual vacuum was to be avoided. At the end of the audience I officially conveyed an invitation to the Pope to address a plenary session of the European Parliament in Strasbourg.

That visit duly took place in 1988 and provided one moment of awkward drama on the floor of the House, involving, almost inevitably, the Reverend Ian Paisley. He was not without supporters in opposing the Pope's visit; the largest political group in Parliament, the Socialists, had only agreed to the invitation on the condition that in protocol terms it was related to the Pope as Head of State of the Vatican and not as Church Leader. But we sensed that, given his known views and past record, Dr Paisley would scarcely pass up such a golden opportunity not only to protest about the visit, but also to engineer a confrontation with the arch-enemy, which would be a world wide media spectacle. The first part of his action passed off smoothly. On the eve of the visit, when the business of the next day was routinely and briefly debated, Dr Paisley took the floor and began to deliver his protest. To the surprise of many in the House and, increasingly, of the Member himself, I allowed him to elaborate on his reasons for objection.

He clearly expected me to cut him off at any moment and therefore raced through his speech at an ever faster gallop. But I had decided to let him have his democratic say - better the day before than on the day itself. Meanwhile I had studied the Rules of Procedure carefully (they were not usually my bedtime reading) and worked out with key members of staff that on the day, assuming Dr Paisley attempted to interrupt the Pope's address, I would issue two clear formal warnings, with reference to the appropriate Rule, then call upon the ushers physically to remove him from the Chamber.

The papal entourage, alerted to what might happen, were understandably nervous, but the Pope himself remained relaxed. I told him that, should an interruption occur, he should simply stop delivering his speech and that I would handle the disturbance. He then delivered himself of a phrase which was to pass into European Parliament folklore: 'OK, my friend Henry, you are the boss.' There was a last minute scare when one of the ushers reported that Dr Paisley was in his place very early and that a clinking noise had been heard emanating from his briefcase. Could this be a chain, with which he would attach himself to the furniture in the Chamber? A messenger was dispatched to fetch wire cutters and the tension mounted.

In the end, everything went according to plan, including, I suspect, Dr Paisley's plans. The Pope was two minutes into his address when the Ulsterman rose and began shouting his opposition at a volume which masked the content. While I was rapidly going through the procedural warnings, he also produced a protest banner, which was subsequently snatched from him by an outraged Otto von Habsburg; but Dr Paisley had several more of them hidden in his poacher's pockets. The ushers, on cue, came for him and out he went, peacefully but scarcely quietly, and the doors of the Chamber closed on him, to the relief of all, including I would guess, Dr Paisley himself.

It was a strange feeling to carry out my official visit to the United Kingdom and to be treated as a VIP visitor from outside. Of course I had known most of the people I was due to meet for years, but my Presidential role provided the opportunity to discuss developments at European level in a new way. A national topic of debate at that moment was the possibility of the UK joining the Exchange Rate Mechanism. The Government mantra on the subject was 'when the time is right'. I must say that, in the light of what they have both since written on the topic, neither Geoffrey Howe, the Foreign Secretary, nor Nigel Lawson, the Chancellor of the Exchequer, gave anything away in their respective analyses of the situation. They were both scrupulously loyal to the Prime Minister's line, even though, as we now know, they were increasingly at war with her over policy on this issue.

My audience with Her Majesty the Queen was an agreeable occasion, which sowed the seeds for a future royal visit to Strasbourg. In my private talk with the Queen in her study, I gently pointed out that she was the only Head of a member state who had not so far addressed a plenary session of the European Parliament. I also expressed the view that such a visit would do more to influence British public opinion in a favourable way than any information campaign we, as an institution, could possibly mount. I would naturally be delighted if she would accept an invitation during my own term of office. Unsurprisingly, the Queen was guarded in her reply and I knew, from various sources, that she had been receiving contrary advice from influential quarters on the other side of St James's Park. It remains a disappointment to me that the Queen did not visit Strasbourg during my presidency, but I was delighted when she eventually did so in May 1992, when she was warmly received by Egon Klepsch, as President, and by the whole House.

Before the audience ended, the Queen asked me for what she termed 'a piece of professional advice.' Was this going to be a question about the CAP and its implications for the royal estates? No, it was not. 'What on earth can one do with Canada geese? They simply eat up the lawns,' said the Queen, pointing down at an offending flock on the edges of the pond in the garden below.

I could go on, reflecting on the many highlights as well as lowlights of my Presidency. Whatever the ups and downs, it was one of the most trying and exciting periods in my life. During my term of office, the European Parliament developed and matured to a unit of real and realistic power, an ever increasing and strong voice in the European decision-making process.

Europe looking out

About three months after the 1979 European Elections the Community signed the second Lomé Convention and agreement with the then 58 ACP (African, Caribbean and Pacific) Countries, which would lead to my second major role in the European Parliament.

Through my work for the IFAP, the International Federation of Agricultural Producers, and COPA the canvas became broader and my interest in the possibility of the inclusion of many countries in Eastern Europe increased accordingly. I always saw the importance of Europe looking out to the rest of the world, knowing as we do that half the world is starving and that we have a responsibility to try to help those countries which are suffering to help themselves.

43

In 1994 I was elected Co-President of the EU-ACP Joint Assembly. This body brings together MEPs from the different political groups who are particularly interested in looking at the problems of developing countries. It also brings together like-minded politicians from Lomé Convention countries far and wide.

At the present time, the participants are seventy-one countries from African, Caribbean and Pacific areas, including South Africa, which joined about a year ago, and, of course, the fifteen countries of the European Union. The ACP countries elect their own Co-President. The Joint Assembly meets twice a year in different parts of the world. One session is held in one of ACP countries, which has the advantage of direct confrontation with a particular problem; during my Co- Presidency always in African countries apart from once in Mauritius. The second annual session takes place in either Brussels, Strasbourg or Luxembourg.

The conference normally lasts four days and concludes with the adoption of Resolutions agreed by all the members of the Assembly and then used to advise the Council of Ministers. The Assembly works very closely with the Commission, since they are responsible for the many technical and aid programmes designed to assist developing countries, and the poorer regions in particular.

The main point of business is to ensure that EU funding is well spent. The funding is to a large extent used by Non-Governmental Organisations, such as Médecins sans Frontières, Oxfam, Christian Aid and other bodies working with great courage in some of the more difficult areas.

The office of Co-President is not just a matter of chairing or presiding over a Joint Conference; that is an aspect of bringing together the various interests. The responsibility also included travelling to the areas to assess where help is most needed. Wherever I went, it was a true learning exercise. Many of the poorer regions are looking towards Europe for assistance, not just in terms of financial or food aid, but also in the form of training to develop their technology, education and healthcare, and to assist with the improvement of peace and security through the promotion of human rights.

This process is carried out under the Lomé Convention, an agreement signed for the first time in 1975 in Lomé, the capital of Togo, between the ACP countries and the European Economic Community as it was then. At that time, the commitment was made by a nine-member EEC, with the objective to promote and expedite the economic, cultural and social development of the ACP countries, all former colonies of the EEC member countries. It was agreed that the Convention would be reviewed at regular intervals, and during my Co-Presidency we were working under Lomé IV. This covered the last decade before the new millennium, when future options for ACP-EU cooperation were to be explored.

During the months leading up to the 1979 Second Convention (Lomé II), the ACP countries started lobbying for separate funds for agriculture, the mainstay of their economies. Their intention was to participate in the decision making process with respect to the management of such a fund, an issue which was deliberated and discussed at great length but it did not necessarily work out in the way that some of them would have hoped. However, the emphasis was on technical development and a technical centre for agriculture that then was created. The Ethiopian Ambassador in one of the EEC countries was very much instrumental in encouraging this decision.

I visited many of the more difficult areas. At the end of the most horrific time that existed in Rwanda, where genocide had been taking place and the war between the different ethnic tribes continued, I went to Rwanda and witnessed the devastation. I met the people who were living in refugee camps, many who had gone over the country borders, wandering the roads and not quite knowing where to go, and I went into Zaire, where some of the camps were created. Seventy to a hundred thousand people living together in one camp, under canvas in rainy weather was an appalling site. My prison visits, for instance in Kigali, were experiences I shall never, ever forget; these prisons were so crowded, that there was not even room to lie down and have a rest, and people had to take it in turns.

The bitterness between the Hutus and the Tutsis was indescribable and this had been festering for many, many years. Thank God that situation has improved but the devastation it caused had effected every aspect of development. I saw the small farms, where there was tremendous potential for the growth of food, that had been left totally neglected, and those who had been farming and living in these areas would probably never go back.

At that time, I realised more than ever the purpose of our involvement; the role of 'Europe looking out' within our agreed responsibility to help. If we look at the total amount of support made available to assist the developing countries under the Lomé Convention by adding the contribution of the currently fifteen member states to the funds provided under the European Aid Programme, the European Union is investing about thirty billion dollars a year into developing countries, which is considerably more than contributed by any other country, or groups of countries, in the world. It is one of our most important functions and yet it is never fully satisfying as one always feels that the progress that has been made is not really what should or could have been achieved

We are continually reminded that the world population could increase or even double by the year 2030. That is an incredible thought, particularly when one considers the surplus of food in many parts of the world as contrasted to the enormous shortages elsewhere. I remember a meeting I once had in Brussels with the President of Uganda, Mr Yoweri Museveni. During lunch, he suddenly turned to me and said:

'I understand you are a farmer?'
'Yes President, I am a farmer'
'So am I a farmer' he said, and continued 'So I suppose

you get one good crop a year, and a good harvest?'
'No President, a farmer never gets a good crop, he
might get a reasonable crop but I've never had what a
farmer would be satisfied to call a good crop,' I replied.
'Well, I often get two harvests or even three harvests,
or two harvests and three crops, so why are you trying
to feed me?'

In fact, he had surplus food in the north of the country
and terrific shortages in the south. In essence, his big
problem was not the production of food for his people but
the distribution of it. We in the West, in the industrialised
countries, tend to think that because we have the technology,
the science, the know-how, the skills and because we can
therefore produce, food aid is the order of the day. What Mr
Museveni was really saying to me was that his country could
grow the stuff too. What they needed from us was the
expertise in order to add value to it, to move it around to
ship it to different areas; it is marketing where the expertise
is needed and fair play in the market place.

But in the face of the multiple challenges that are
brought about by globalisation and as we see the failure of
ministers to deal with these issues at the World Trade
Organisation meeting in Seattle, we recognise that if we will
have what is termed 'globalisation' and 'free trade'
throughout the world, then it has to be 'fair trade' between
countries.

Rethinking free and fair

Developing countries need all the support they can get,
both from multilateral and from bilateral donors to sustain
their effort towards the gradual opening up of markets and
their integration into the world economy. With its
combination of aid and trade provisions, the positive
relationship between the Union and the seventy-one ACP

countries provides a comprehensive and potentially powerful operational framework within which to achieve this.

The operational practice of the ACP-EU partnership has however shown its limitations and its weak points. Each group will have to make fundamental political choices regarding the type of cooperation and agreement it wants beyond the year 2000. The Commission is working on this, recognising the need for change and putting forward proposals to deal with the challenges which exist and the options for a new partnership. The official position of the ACP countries is only beginning to emerge; naturally their concerns and particular wishes will take time to crystalise.

The creation of the World Trade Organisation in January 1995 had serious implications for EU trade arrangements for current and future trade with developing countries. The most immediate issue is the basic incompatibility of the Lomé trade provisions with the rules of WTO. The way in which EU-ACP member states develop their trade relations post 2000 will be of obvious concern to the WTO and its members. Any proposal on this front can expect microscopic inspection by those who feel that their interests may be at stake.

The new context therefore requires a radical rethink of developmental policy. Development must be seen as a whole; building new schools is of no use if there are no roads to get children to them and if there are no trained teachers, books and equipment. Establishing banks and financial institutions without proper supervision will lead to chaos and without a clear strategy, piecemeal policies are recipes for disaster.

Our work will not end for as long as nations are divided between rich and poor. Three billion people still live on less than two dollars a day; one hundred and thirty million children of school age get no formal education; 1.5 billion people do not have access to clean water; two billion people are without sewage and water facilities, yet whilst international markets are unstable and the needs of the poor increase, overseas development assistance is being reduced.

This in my opinion is a foolish, short-term approach, but this does not mean that Europe's future relations with the seventy-one ACP states can be dismissed. On the contrary we are bound together by common history and by a moral duty to help the world's poor. However, the developing countries must understand that basic democratic principles underpin economic growth.

Corruption free government, the rule of law, effective judicial systems, proper financial structures, and above all - a good basic education based on ability, not on ethnic or family connections, all these factors create prosperity and stability.

Poverty and conflict go hand in hand, often leading to famine and war. The issue of debt relief must be tackled although we must be careful not to subsidise corruption and profligacy in doing so. Developed nations must stop stifling those economies that are struggling to succeed. The new millennium should mark the new beginning in North-South relations. Economic freedom must cease to be used as an excuse for economic exploitation. We must prevent smaller poor nations from being isolated as the big beasts seek to carve up the world's economy. In short, we must remember our neighbours.

Naturally, people often query. In 1994, European development aid cost the three hundred and seventy million citizens of the fifteen EU member states 64 ECU each (1 ECU = 1 euro = approx. 60p). However as this amount represents the arithmetic average of annual global expenditure for development by the EU (15% by the EU jointly on the one hand and 85% by the member states on the other) it could vary significantly from one member state to the next.

The burden was naturally smaller for the citizens of poorer countries and larger for residents of the more prosperous states. For example, each Dane spent 222 ECU each to support development, whilst the British paid only 43 ECU each and the Portuguese 25 ECU.

The 64 ECU that the average European contributed to development is more or less equivalent to the cost of a concert ticket and it represents some 10% of what a one-pack-a-day smoker spends on cigarettes in a year.

In 1994 the share of this 64 ECU attributed to management costs by the European Commission, amounted to 5 ECU, less than the price of a cinema ticket. It is a small price to pay to give a future to millions of the poorest people on earth.

The investment appears even wiser when we consider that it often contributes to the development of our own society as well. Under co-operation agreements the ACP countries regularly call on European enterprises that produce goods or provide services.

In or *out* of Europe

Although I decided not to seek re-election in June 1999, my interest in matters European, and Britain's role and level of participation within the European Union has not diminished and never will. However, in February this year I had an experience which left me somewhat puzzled. I witnessed the nationwide launch of the 'Britain in Europe' campaign, a cross party initiative which I support, believing that the depth of our involvement in the European Union is too important an issue to be used as a political football.

I am aware of the current political climate, of the ever growing anxiety in our country to cut the umbilical cord with Europe, and of the ongoing arguments from all sides, many of them comfortably hidden under an umbrella of national pride. And so, for a moment and as a thought experiment, I asked myself why should I not change my tune. I am British and I am proud of it. Why Britain *in* Europe? Why bother? Since so many apparently intelligent people think that it is possible for Britain to turn its back on the commitments and agreements made in the context of its international relationships, why should I not review my ardent belief that it is in the interest of our country to be part of Europe? Indeed, why should we not campaign for Britain *out* of Europe? Or better still, Britain outside Europe, nowhere near it, a million miles away?

There would be no interference from Brussels. We would live in peace. There would be no more tinpot officials closing down our bring-and-buy sales and allowing foreigners to over-fish our waters. We would have time to concentrate on what is really needed in trade and industry and would have to endure no further lecturing about the benefits of a single market or a single currency, or a single anything else. We would be a country brave and free, beholden to nobody. We would not be infected by continental rabies, not by Romantic poetry, not by Germanic angst. More importantly, we would be totally independent. We would be self-sufficient in goods, services, dreams and ideas and illusions. And we could eat our prawn-flavoured crisps and drink our warm beer in peace.

We would not have to justify our customs officials, our police powers, nor our tabloid newspapers. We would not have to play and lose against nations who don't play cricket. Furthermore, we would be able to protect our people from foreign exploitation so that only they could take the jobs offered by British companies. Nobody else would be allowed to invest in Britain. We would become the first European tiger economy, re-equipped with dentures and plastic claws. So I wonder, why not support a Britain out of Europe campaign?

In 1975, the United Kingdom had its first national referendum. The Government - a Labour Government - had decided after many twists and turns to recommend a 'yes' vote for the UK to stay in Europe, a recommendation supported by the majority of the Conservative Party. The so-called 'eurosceptics' were the extreme Left and the extreme Right, including the Communists and the Fascists. Abroad, Britain's friends (including their colonies and ex-colonies) wanted us to stay in. Britain's enemies (including the Soviet Union and the Comecon countries) wanted us to get out.

What is new today? The extreme Right and the extreme Left still want us to leave. Our friends abroad still want us to stay in and our enemies still want us to get out. Moreover, other things have not changed either; we still suffer from scepticism, a political plague now sustained by ignorance. What we wanted to come about has not. What we thought would not happen, has. What we believed in has turned out to be incredible, what we doubted trustworthy. The old lessons still have not been learned; extremists are extremists, wherever they come from, politically or geographically. Why bother?

The answer to this question lies in my strong belief that what we can do together within the European Union is far more effective than we could achieve on our own. In the light of the increased difficulties of the developing world and looking at recent events and the deep disillusionment of the people in Zimbabwe, I believe that we must re-double our efforts to minimise future disasters and to help countries all over the world to get to grips with their deep underlying problems.

More Europe?

Faced with this complicated and difficult scenario, many people doubt that we can achieve our goals within the framework of European integration. But my experience persuades me they are wrong. Paradoxically, I find whenever I travel outside Europe, that the rest of the world is more impressed than we are by what we have already achieved and that people on other continents look to us with confidence - and not a little envy - expecting us to meet the challenges successfully.

Those within Europe who take a more optimistic approach believe that it will be necessary to have 'more Europe' than in the past in order to get to grips with the problems which confront us. I agree with that view but with two important reservations.

Firstly, 'more Europe' should not mean further far-reaching institutional novelties; we still need to absorb and consolidate the institutional changes introduced in Maastricht and Amsterdam. What we need are organisational and managerial changes to make the workings of the Union more transparent and efficient.

Secondly, I believe that 'more Europe' will only be possible if we in the European Union can get to grips with the most pressing problem of all, namely that of bringing the people of Europe together and sharing ideas, yet with mutual respect for our cultural differences. After all, other cultures, the Germans, the French, the Italians are just as peculiar and idiosyncratic to us as we are to them. These aspects have to be understood, appreciated and accommodated in order for a European-based, universal programme for unbiased cooperation and peace to work.

Much lip service has been paid to this objective, but I am not at all convinced that it has been pursued in practical ways with anything like the dedication that is necessary. Indeed, even at the present stage of development within Europe, we have a potentially dangerous situation. When one looks at public opinion polls throughout the Union, one cannot escape the fact that amongst the population at large, the degree of ignorance, indifference or even hostility regarding European integration is alarmingly high. We certainly cannot be complacent about public attitudes to the European Parliament and, by extension, to all the institutions of the Union. This would be a major problem even if the Union's ambitions and needs were restricted to maintaining the status-quo. But to attempt to move forward over the next few years in the ways which will be called for without first solving this problem could well be folly.

This might sound like a gloomy statement coming from someone with my known attitudes and track record and I hasten to add that I am not in the least gloomy, since I am convinced that the problem of public acceptance can indeed be solved.

The solution does not lie in any 'quick-fix' or by sole means of a massive information campaign, useful though such a campaign may be.

What we need for the European citizen is a guide to who should be doing what, at which level, within the European Union, whether at the European centre, nationally or regionally. And the underlying principle must be that the European centre should only be handling matters which can only appropriately be dealt with there.

In that regard, I believe that such a detailed guide would do much to calm the fears of those who believe that European integration means that all Europe will somehow be run from Brussels. I have no doubt that objective efficiency will decree that only a small proportion of legislative and administrative action should actually be carried out from the centre.

Member states' governments must play a more active role in conveying to their national audiences a positive message about European affairs. It is tempting for all of them to present themselves as champions of the national interest and to blame any setbacks on villainous and faceless 'Brussels bureaucrats.'

Hence even the vocabulary of European debate in most member state parliaments is couched in military terms, with ministerial 'victories' and the 'successful resistance to attacks from the Commission or the conspiracies of other member states.'

I recognise, of course, that there is a fundamental problem here for national governments and indeed national parliamentary opposition. It is a fact of life that progress within Europe can only be achieved by the gradual redistribution of powers and responsibilities between the various levels of authority: European, national, regional and local. It is also clear that in the context of that redistribution, it is the nation state that is likely to be required to give up more competences, either towards the European centre or to regional and local authorities.

Yet at the same time, in the present state of European evolution, the power of ultimate decision remains at the level of national governments, whose natural instinct is to avoid being the 'victim' of this process. No one can be surprised at that. However, it must be borne in mind that, quite apart from the process of European integration, which flows from the Treaty of Rome and its successors, the nation state as hitherto understood is bound to mutate. This is due to the fact of globalisation; in our shrinking and ever more interdependent world, the classic concept of the nation state is simply no longer sustainable in the longer term. Change has become inevitable. Furthermore, the opportunities provided within the framework of the European Union mean that the nation states of Europe can mutate to face the challenges of globalisation in an orderly and mutually beneficial way. It is that which makes our Union the envy of so much of the rest of the world.

Identity and sovereignty

My next point is linked to the mutation of the nation state which I have just described. I refer to a distinction which should be drawn between the concept of 'national sovereignty' on the one hand, and 'national identity' on the other. Clearly, there are points at which these two concepts impinge with each other. For example, the history of national sovereignty in any given country is also part of the development of the national identity of its people. However, I believe that it is extremely important for the citizens of Europe to be aware of the ways in which these concepts differ from one another. To illustrate what I mean, let me cite the extreme example of the many citizens in this country who express reservations about Europe because they say that they have no wish to become 'someone else' and that their strong desire is to remain themselves. How often I have heard the cry 'I am British and I want to stay British.'

What such people are actually expressing is a desire to protect their national identity, an aspiration I fully support, but unfortunately they confuse it with the 'sovereignty' issue.

There is a great need to convince the electorate at large that in a modern world, quite apart from considerations of European integration, the idea of complete national sovereignty, as it would have applied for example in the late 19th century, is simply no longer tenable; again, this is due to the forces of globalisation and interdependency which I have already touched upon, not just to European integration. For a country to be completely 'sovereign' would mean that it was completely isolated.

In any international agreement, those countries participating give up a piece, however great or small, of their sovereignty. Any action taken in the sphere governed by the agreement must take account of the rights of the other participants. Clearly, within the European Union this process of pooling sovereignty has already reached an advanced degree. But the real question to be posed is not to what degree has sovereignty been sacrificed; rather, the key political question is what benefits have we derived from this pooling of sovereignty? In my mind the answer in each of our member states is resoundingly positive.

Special reference should be made here, I believe, to the role of national parliaments within the European Union. Too often in the past, national parliaments have been thought of as existing in a state of rivalry to the European Parliament. I have never believed that; I see their respective roles as being complementary.

Having served as a European parliamentarian for twenty years, I strongly advocate a more powerful role for all national parliaments within the EU system. This role should be chronologically different to that of the European Parliament. By this I mean that national parliaments should structure their business in such a way as to familiarise themselves with European legislation at the earliest possible stage - that is to say at the stage of the formulation of national policy. In other words, national parliaments should be able to make an informed input into the determination of *their* ministers' policy guidelines on any particular subject *before* the minister goes off to Brussels for negotiations at the European level. In many member states that would call for quite profound changes in the way Parliament is organised and indeed in the relationship between government and parliament, for everyone's benefit.

Turning now to the concept of national identity, I do not think that anyone could argue that since 1958 the French have become less French, the German less German, the Italians less Italian or indeed the British less British. It is true that we have borrowed from one another such everyday items as traditional foods; we exchange top level footballers; we trade more with one another than ever before and our homes are full of products manufactured all across the Union. By and large we know more about one another than our forefathers did and we have far greater opportunities to visit one another's countries. We have therefore for all these reasons become more Europeanised in an enriching way. But we have not been pushed towards conforming to some theoretical standard 'European citizen'; neither has any national identity become dominant in the way in which the efforts of the past to create Europe by force inevitably led. No one has the ambition to interfere with any of the national or indeed regional identities encompassed in the European Union.

On the contrary, I believe that with a clear application of subsidiarity, national, regional and local identities will have enhanced opportunities to flourish and to enrich the lives of individual citizens.

I believe that many critics of the European ideal would be greatly reassured if this point were fully understood. Therefore, it is important that even greater emphasis is now placed on research into the essence of national identity and how best this can be accommodated within the EU framework.

For example, academics should examine the possible differences between identity as a subconscious protection mechanism and identity as the source of stubborn patriotism, or indeed xenophobia. Scientific awareness of such matters might lead to a better understanding of how this complex factor can best be taken into account in the process of European integration.

It is fascinating to note that consideration is now being given to subsidiarity and identity, in that, against the background of devolutionary developments in Scotland, Wales and Northern Ireland, the English are beginning to contemplate afresh their own identity and to ponder on whether they should demand a national parliament or regional assemblies, in order to cater for their own particular needs. I have said that national governments bear a particular responsibility for putting across the European message to their respective publics, even though in the long run the nation state may 'lose out,' so to speak, in the direction of both Europe and of the regions.

It is true that European integration cannot be achieved by vision alone, but it is equally true that it cannot be achieved without the positive advocacy of the leaders of the member states.

We need to hear again voices like those of the Founding Fathers, spelling out to the peoples of Europe the advantages of our common Union. I am convinced that success will only be achieved through a combination of managerial efficiency throughout the institutions on the one hand and, on the other, a renewed vision of the Union enthusiastically conveyed by national leaders.

To picture today's problems in historical context, I shall conclude with a quotation from one of Plato's Dialogues with an old Athenian in his *12th Book of Laws* (400 BC) in which he refers to The Good State in its Intercourse with the World:

'The refusal to receive others and to allow
their own citizens to go to other places is utterly

impossible, and to the rest of the world it is likely to appear ruthless and uncivilised; we call the practice by the name of xenelasia or banishment of strangers, which is a hard word, and is descriptive of hard and morose ways, as men think. And to be thought or not to be thought of well by the rest of the world is no light matter.'

A Voice for Cultural Diversity at the Heart of Europe

Carole Tongue

Victory in a marginal seat

'Now I know why you are such a pro-European,' exclaimed Barbara Castle on a walk halfway up a Tyrolean mountain. She and I were on a German language course and she had asked me about my family. My background, I explained, is both staunchly socialist and very internationalist. With at least four different nationalities in my family, and a mother and father whose families had both adopted refugees during the Second World War, I have always felt very European. My stepfather visited Vienna with an ILP (Independent Labour Party) delegation in 1931. On his return he lobbied Jimmy Maxton MP to help bring two Jewish friends to London. I only knew them as Steffie and Charles but later I understood the importance of what my stepfather had done. In addition, my own father was Director of an international organisation in Switzerland and it always seemed normal that one should work with people from different cultures.

Sensing that my future was going to be in public service at a European level I studied French and Government at Loughborough University, with a strong emphasis on European politics. I then spent two summer seasons working in France perfecting my French – something I've been very glad of ever since. Not really wishing to return to Britain, I worked temporarily in Luxembourg and decided one day to walk into the European Parliament to ask if they had any openings for employment. One Robert Schuman scholarship was vacant for British occupancy. I applied and won it, starting in September 1979. I was completely overjoyed, and felt as if I'd come home.

After preparing answers to Parliamentarians' written questions, I produced a report on the response of the European Community to youth unemployment which I hoped would inform policy-making. In March 1980 I took up the job of secretarial and administrative assistant to David Blackman, the Deputy Secretary General of the Socialist Group. I believed it would lead to more challenging opportunities in the future. Being in a European Socialist environment felt like home. The post gave me an invaluable insight into the workings of the Parliament and the Socialist Group, the political cast at that time, the policy issues at stake, and the opportunities and constraints that existed. At the same time, I was becoming gradually more and more disappointed and distressed by the negativity of Labour Party policy on Europe, which culminated in the massive vote for withdrawal at the 1982 Party conference. Following that decision Michael Foot and Eric Heffer came to address the Socialist Group. The forceful contribution of heavyweight MEPs, particularly German members who had suffered under the Nazis, was unforgettable as they pleaded with the British Labour Party not to opt out of the European Community, but to join with other European comrades in moving it in a socialist direction. That appeal had a tremendous effect on me and served to reinforce my determination to change Labour Party European policy.

In mid-1983 I found myself in the hemicycle bar in Strasbourg with John Palmer of *The Guardian*, Alan Osbourne of *The Daily Telegraph* and John Wyles of the *Financial Times*. I was expressing my anger about Labour's anti European policy. As I banged my fist on the bar, I was greeted with an almost unanimous chorus of the three men saying: 'Don't just stand there, STAND as a candidate for MEP.' John Palmer then reached out his hand to shake mine and said 'I put a bet on it, you'll be elected this time next year.' This boosted my confidence to enter the European political arena. I knew it would be a challenge as I had limited recent experience of the Labour Party or of local government enjoyed by many other MEPs. I discussed my future with David Blackman, who himself was standing as a candidate in Coventry. He was enthusiastic about my standing. Whether I was selected or not, by standing I would have the opportunity to say to Labour Party members why Britain's future lay inside the EC.

My selection speech was blunt, and extremely visceral. Taking a gamble, I spoke from the heart. It was easy to be caustic about prevailing anti-European views in the Labour Party. I joked that there were a few pages of the Treaty of Rome which some of the more vociferous anti-EC critics obviously hadn't read. I argued that Labour's place was firmly inside the European boat, from where we could paddle it in our political direction. Fired up by my mother's part-time work experience, I spelled out the importance of winning equality for part-time workers, and of obtaining enhanced rights of parental and maternity leave across Europe to allow people to combine family and work responsibilities. I spoke out for the right of workers in multinational companies such as Ford at Dagenham - which of course was in the London East constituency where I was seeking selection - to take their place as participants within a system of European industrial democracy such as has now been achieved in the form of the European Works Councils. These aims I argued were worth fighting for not only at a national level, but also in Europe, where we had comrades and allies who shared our values and objectives. That working people must unite across frontiers to achieve common goals of social justice, economic prosperity and a sustainable environment in a multinational economy was my basic message.

To my delight, I won the nomination, beating a number of well known activists in the process. Had it been a year earlier, I wouldn't have been successful. As it was, in early 1984, it seemed people were eager for an excuse to think the previously unthinkable on Europe. The first problem to be faced was to find an agent. There was difficulty in getting anyone to come forward, and the first offer was from someone entirely inappropriate. Martin Sachs then took over, a very able man, without whose commitment I would never have been successful. We spent six weeks campaigning across nine different constituencies, allotting about four days to each. We approached the task very methodically, analysing each constituency to work out the best place to meet people. Of course there was the odd mishap. I remember Roland Boyes MP coming to help my campaign in Barkingside, Ilford and there being hardly a shopper in sight!

I owe an enormous debt of gratitude to a number of Labour Party members who were resolutely loyal and supportive to me over the 15 years I was in the European Parliament. Vic and Floss Rusha, Tom Horlock, Amarjit Singh, Alan Thake and Pat and Pete Dedman to name but a few. They never failed to attend every European Constituency Labour Party (ECLP) meeting or to campaign vigorously in every European election. They constantly showed enormous commitment to the European socialist cause. Their Euro enthusiasm inspired many other party members.

Being a young pro-European woman who was not from a traditional stream of the Labour movement, I attracted a degree of media attention. Certainly the local press were very interested, as was local radio. Martin Linton of *The Guardian* wrote a half page profile with a picture of me emerging from a shop in Dagenham, fish and chips in hand. He forecast we would win London East.

After the article even more local activists joined the campaign. Our likely success gave them something to really go out and focus on and fight for. For activists in Wanstead and Woodford, I was proud to be the first ever Labour politician they had elected.

The day we won in London East, the local newspaper carried the amusing headline 'Bionic Carole Goes to Europe.' I remember the count, where the sitting Tory MEP was beaten by a young twenty-eight year old, something very unexpected for an eminent barrister. Looking back, a number of factors worked in our favour. The constituency was one which was always going to be marginal, and which had not been well contested by the Labour Party in 1979. I was a young, energetic and enthusiastic pro-European at the helm of a very positive campaign which succeeded in invigorating and enthusing people at a time when many were already disillusioned by the performance of the Conservative Government. Finally, it helped being a local person who had lived over 20 years previously in different parts of the London East constituency. People felt that I was one of them with an understanding of their concerns and the problems of the area. Local people were also ready to hear a positive message on Europe and register an anti-Tory vote.

Settling into the job

It was unexpected, and very sudden. To have gone so quickly from being a humble, behind the scenes administrative assistant to a front line politician with a public profile represented an amazing life change. The transition was greeted with delight by many people, particularly former female colleagues of mine in the Parliament, who saw me as a helpful role model. I was jubilant and awestruck at finding myself in the job of my dreams. At the same time, I felt an enormous sense of responsibility to help in moving the Labour Party towards a more pro-European stance. Delivering something tangible from the European Union to my constituency and London as a whole was also a top priority.

Nothing could be achieved on my own. From the very beginning I was most fortunate to have a local woman activist, Tessa Jones, working with me as an administrative secretary. She stayed with me for 10 years as the most hardworking and loyal member of staff one could ever have. Recalling an anti-cruise missile demonstration in 1981 in Brussels, I remembered one person on the march and with whom I had shared views and values - Fred Hasson who was working at the time for the London Hazards Centre. I was pleased he agreed to be my political advisor. His experience, political nous and good relations with the trade union movement inspired my work. I owe much to Fred and Tessa. They were patient, insightful, hardworking and often long-suffering as I bombarded them with ideas and the work necessary to achieve our multiple aims.

From 1984 I lived with my dear Parisian friend Huguette Vos when I was in Brussels for committee meetings. I enjoyed meeting her Belgian friends whom we regularly entertained at her house outside Brussels. Once again I revelled in having access to a different cultural perspective. Huguette nurtured me like a mother. Her frank and honest advice and support was invaluable.

It was somewhat intimidating at first being surrounded by experienced MEPs, and *éminences grises* from so many different nation states. Their skill and expertise was clearly a resource to be tapped into, and I never hesitated to seek their advice. I quickly made friends and allies within the British Labour Group. Two people whom I got to know very early on were Joyce Quin MEP and John Tomlinson MEP. Both sat near me during long voting sessions. I am grateful for their patience with my questions and for the ideas we shared. I was drawn immediately to Glyn Ford, another MEP and a thinker with a worldview. He was a tad more sceptical about the European Union than me, but we became firm friends. I remember sitting with him in a café in Florence and discussing what the European Parliament should do about racism and xenophobia. He went on to conduct a vigorous campaign leading to an EU Solemn Declaration and the Observatory Against Racism and Xenophobia. I got on famously with many colleagues from other countries also.

I became good friends with Vera Squarcialupi, an Italian communist who brought me presents of homemade fig jam and spoke passionately about protecting the environment and saving the wolf population in Europe from complete extinction. Still a close friend today, Luciana Castellina MEP from a small left Italian party became an inspirational soulmate and mentor. Dutch MEP Hedy d'Ancona was bright, intelligent, and so much fun. She chaired the European Parliament's Women's Committee from 1984-89 and went on to be Dutch culture minister from 1989-94. We shared values and ideas, particularly on policies to combat drug abuse.

There was a lot to pick up in my initial weeks, from what to speak on and where, to how to write a press release. I learnt from the doggedness, determination and integrity of my more experienced colleagues, from their ability to stand up for their beliefs and not be intimidated by the opposition, and from the way in which they handled relations with the Commission and sought to influence others. Barbara Castle was an inspiration and a political mentor, even if we did not always agree on the future of Europe at this time. Her example taught me the value of meticulous research, and that it was wholly appropriate to plan out one's speeches on paper in advance. It was very important to be as clear and succinct as possible, since one almost invariably had just two or three minutes to speak in the Parliament. It certainly prevented one from boring the audience!

At the constituency level, I was learning very fast how best to reach the electorate. Again, I gained a lot of useful guidance from watching my colleagues. What kind of events were they organising in their constituencies and were they writing a column for the local press? Visits to local schools, trades unions, pensioners' clubs and voluntary sector projects became a priority. John Smith MP, then Labour Party Leader, addressed a 500 strong European conference in East Ham Town Hall. Workshops brought party activists, trades unions and the voluntary sector together to develop European policy ideas. A cross-channel rail link company paid for a stand and helped sponsor the meeting. The event was a huge success and raised the profile of what Labour was achieving in the EC among local people.

It was wonderful to find oneself taking part in policy-making alongside colleagues from other countries. The differences in approach between the nationalities were often quite marked. One particularly vivid example of this was serving on the 1985 EP Committee of Inquiry into Drug Addiction. I agreed (and still do), with the Dutch harm reduction approach to drug abuse. Very few MEPs chose to agree with me despite police and other testimony supporting my scepticism about the contemporary 'war on drugs' policies. As a result Hedy d'Ancona MEP, Heinke Salisch MEP and I wrote a minority report advocating a radical change in policies.

In general terms the range of 'national personalities' was fascinating. The Dutch could be blunt sometimes to the point of giving offence, but in a way which could really move things forward. Then there were the Italians, whose passion and charm was irresistible, but whom one often felt like giving the odd shake in order to pin them down to something practical and specific. I soon learnt that Italian vagueness was part of a very subtle diplomacy and often very effective in avoiding alienating anyone. My German colleagues offered insights from their long tradition of social democracy which were immensely valuable and enlightening, but they could occasionally show a lack of flexibility in their thinking. Speaking fluent French and being a devoted Francophile soon endeared me to many French MEPs, particularly those on the Left. I share the French passion for securing cultural diversity and sovereignty for all regions and nations.

Compromise is essential in the European Parliament, and members from countries with a tradition of broad coalition in government were of course well practised at the art. One learnt about getting together with Green, Christian Democrat or Liberal members and finding a way forward, whilst retaining as much as one's original idea as possible. I was very fortunate in this respect to be on the Environment, Consumer Protection and Public Health committee, which was a model of how to achieve cross-party compromise, and which produced excellent reports as a result. The then Chair, Ken Collins MEP, would always remind audiences that 60% of our amendments formed part of final legislation, a record unachievable by national backbench MPs. Important here is that MEPs had considerable influence over the salient issues of pollution; consumer protection and achieving sustainable development.

My French and German, and later on my Spanish, were an enormous advantage. I was very grateful to my mother for encouraging me to learn them. It was a joy to communicate directly with all MEPs without needing an interpreter. I think my language skills, which at that time were quite atypical for a British MEP, enhanced my popularity and credibility within the body of the Socialist Group as a whole, and enabled me to reach parts of the Parliament which others couldn't reach. One always gained respect from colleagues if one could address them in their own language. I always tried to do so. Even if discussing car exhaust emissions or coal-fired power stations in German was a challenge, the fact that I'd made the initial effort made a huge difference!

Fighting for a pro-European Labour policy

I joined the European Parliament at a time when the British Labour Group was bitterly divided. First there were the diehard anti-Europeans, like Bob Cryer and Les Huckfield. Second, there were those who, although constructively critical were sceptical in their attitude towards the European Union. Finally there were those, including myself, who were constructively critical but at the same time very pro-European. These differences caused enormous tensions within the Group. I was treated with suspicion and even outright hostility by some members, on account of my pro-European stance and my former background in the Parliament. It was wearing. In order to preserve my sanity,

I sought refuge in my friendships and work collaboration with other members of the Socialist Group, as did other pro-Europeans.

But I was always fired up by the fact I had been selected and elected as a pro-European candidate. Thankfully, change was in the air. In 1982 Barbara Castle MEP wrote an article in the *New Statesman* suggesting that the Labour Party should reevaluate its policy of withdrawal, setting out instead a positive socialist agenda for the development of the Community. This marked a huge shift, and had a clear impact on the whole Labour Movement. Then in 1984 Barbara continued to lead the British Labour Group for a further eighteen months, providing much needed critically constructive pro-European leadership. In 1986, however, the pro-European campaign to change party policy on Europe suffered a temporary setback with the election of the anti-European Alf Lomas MEP to the leadership. A group of us at this time had been thinking about ways in which we could move the debate on. Anita Pollack, then Barbara Castle's Political Assistant, and I had already entered into discussions with John Lloyd of the *New Statesman* and Frances Morrell, former Leader of ILEA, concerning this. It was decided that we would organise a series of meetings, supported by the *New Statesman* and the Friedrich Ebert Stiftung, the German Social Democrat Foundation, to which we would invite members of the shadow cabinet and prominent socialists from other countries for discussion. We hoped that this would prompt the Labour leadership to reconsider the Party's policy on Europe. The strategy worked well. I can recall Bryan Gould, in conversation with two politicians from two different Italian left-wing parties, wriggling quite uncomfortably at what they were saying to him. He realised perhaps that his anti-European views were deeply visceral and didn't stand up to rational scrutiny. Sadly this would keep him from serious consideration as a potential Labour Party leader.

Meanwhile, the pro-Europeans in the British Labour Group were always seeking to explain and educate their

European general management committees back in their constituencies about the nature and validity of the work that they were doing, and the value of European collaborative endeavour. A number of us found that one of the most effective ways of influencing the attitude of Party members towards Europe was to invite across a prominent European socialist to address our European Constituency Labour Party. This had a powerful effect. Local party members heard from foreign MEPs who were just as devout socialists as they were, appealing to them to join in a common socialist endeavour at the European level. Both Hedy d'Ancona MEP and Philip de Coene MEP came to Ilford and entranced local party people with their spirited vision of a truly democratic socialist Europe.

1988 was a turning point in the British European debate. Jacques Delors made a keynote speech to the Trades Union Congress (TUC) in Bournemouth. I had gone to see him in the spring of that year, to express my concern about potential redundancies arising out of the developments in the single market at that time. During our meeting he mentioned that he had received invitations to address both the Australian Labour Party Congress and the British TUC, and asked me which I thought he should accept. Without hesitation, I said that he should go to the TUC. This advice was borne out by events. His speech turned out to be an historic event, which enabled the TUC to adopt a new agenda on Europe. As a European Trade Unionist, socialist, and President of the European Commission, Jacques Delors' call to the TUC Congress to join with other socialists in pursuing a common European agenda was immensely powerful. Most of the European Parliamentary Labour Party (EPLP) were delighted at the change of TUC policy and felt that things were finally shifting in a pro-European direction. From this moment on, the Party moved very clearly under Neil Kinnock towards a constructive pro-European agenda, culminating in the very positive and successful 1989 European election campaign.

Visiting abroad

I must have been mad! I accepted two important visits in 1985, to two countries arguably living through the most intractable political situations outside Northern Ireland, namely Israel and South Africa.

I was brought up in a Quaker-pacifist context, and my parents had been members of the CND for as long as I could remember. It was thus an honour when Bruce Kent, the leader of the CND, telephoned me as a friend and a colleague to ask if I could replace him at a meeting in Johannesburg organised by 'END Conscription,' a campaign of mostly white young men who were opposed to being called up into the armed forces of the apartheid regime.

After my first ever club class flight overnight to Johannesburg, I arrived excited but full of trepidation. Here I was to support a dissident movement, in the midst of a state of emergency. Guns were just another piece of luggage on the airport turntable, something that I'd never seen before. To say I was heading for a new experience was a slight understatement. In my handbag I had wads of anti-apartheid articles. They were banned material in South Africa, and if I were stopped, they could get me into trouble, even as an MEP. But I steeled myself with the knowledge that I must get such information through to encourage those fighting apartheid, and to reassure oppressed South Africans that the rest of the world really did care about their plight and were campaigning for the demise of apartheid.

I stayed with some young white students in Johannesburg, who were very excited that they had found a vehicle to oppose the regime, and thrilled that people like myself had agreed to come to support their campaign. At the meeting, I was deeply honoured to share a platform with the great Desmond Tutu. It was very moving to bring greetings from the British peace movement and from fellow Europeans opposed to the apartheid regime. It was with humility I transmitted a message of hope and courage to people living through such turbulent and tragic times. The courage and sheer enormity of the anti-apartheid struggle within South Africa was truly humbling, and made my own political battles seem puny by comparison. Everyone present was shocked and saddened at hearing that one of the speakers from the UDF had been murdered on the way to the meeting. That wasn't something that happened very often in Britain or Western Europe. Politically we didn't know we were born, I thought to myself. We had no real appreciation of this degree of everyday tragedy.

I travelled out one day with a young white woman to a settlement in Bophutaswana where two hundred people were using a single water tap. I remember staring in disbelief at this spectacle, almost speechless in front of people so deprived of human dignity and respect. At the same time one felt optimism that my companion and others like her were doing their utmost to alleviate appalling living conditions. On another occasion, I went into Soweto, against the advice of my friends, to hear Helen Joseph speak in a church there. It was one of the most moving experiences of my life, to see that small, fragile old lady, openly challenging the powerful white regime with such guts and determination. She raised the roof with her words and inspiration. The singing that day was marvellous, and the courage of the people there quite incredible. I don't think I felt unsafe, but I certainly moved about in a state of trepidation, knowing myself to be in a situation of turmoil and considerable potential violence.

I visited Cape Town and went with a Liberal Member of Parliament to the site of the massacre at Lange Uitenhaag. She was dressed in a tweed skirt and a Victorian-style blouse which looked deeply incongruous against the corrugated-iron slum in which we stood, almost ankle deep in mud. She showed me the bullet holes where people had been mown down, and we stopped to talk with families whose members had been killed. She was doing all that she could to help them, giving them support and legal advice, and helping to bring independent witness to bear. Suddenly down one of the avenues of clogged mud there thundered huge armoured personnel carriers full of young conscripts. I shall never forget the way she stood there with her hands on her hips, asking them what they thought they were doing terrifying the townships in this way, and challenging them to come down from their machine and engage in discussion with us. We got into our car, and went elsewhere to talk to another group of the inhabitants, but the army refused to leave us alone, always following not far behind. They were clearly disturbed by the presence of two white women, reasonably smartly dressed, in the township, and couldn't work out what we were doing there. I've since learned that the MP who took me that day was killed in a car crash, but I have my doubts if it was really an accident. She was a thorn in the side of the establishment and a very brave woman indeed.

I saw my trip as an opportunity to record the direct witness of a number of different individuals, taking tapes of my conversations out of the country as up-to-the-minute evidence of the situation. Since South Africa was not one of my areas of expertise, it was clearly best to pass the information on to others who could make good use of it. I gave my taped interviews to Commissioner Claude Cheysson, who was shortly due to go on an official visit to South Africa. He was delighted by the range of the people I had managed to interview, and vowed to make sure that he was given the opportunity to meet similar people. I also debriefed members of the anti-apartheid movement, and wrote a report which I passed on to MPs and MEPs whom I knew to have a particular interest in South Africa. I believe that my information was put to good use, all serving to help keep up the pressure on the apartheid regime. The EU had a good record with respect to its attitude to apartheid in South Africa.

My second visit was as part of the official European Parliament delegation to Israel. I chose to put my name down for this particular delegation because in East London I represented one of the largest Jewish populations of any constituency. It was important get to know and understand the situation in the Middle East better, and to develop as balanced a view of the situation as possible.

The visit brought home to me just how intractable the situation in the Middle East was at that time. It was a powerful experience living in the midst of such an apparent impasse. I can remember waking up at night agonising as to how progress could ever be achieved. How could there ever be peaceful coexistence of Jews and Arabs in the region? I came to realise for the first time just how strongly many Jewish people felt about the need to have their own state, and to defend it vigorously in the face of external threat. I also learnt that the Jewish population, far from being a great monolith sharing similar views, in fact encompassed a wide variety of opinion. Meeting with Shulamit Aloni, for example, the great left-wing peace campaigner, showed me that there were Israelis who did see a different way forward, and did not feel frightened by the prospect of working together with their so-called adversaries towards a negotiated and amicable peace settlement. David Hare's 'Via Doloroso' brought back powerful memories of my visit and of Shulamit Aloni. Ten years on and she was still as passionate a campaigner as ever. Similarly, I also met a wide range of opinion within the Arab population, too. Inspirational peace makers on both sides gave me hope.

Our delegation visit enabled us to collect hard evidence from a wide range of people, which could then be used to inform the policy of the European Commission, the shadow cabinet and others. For my part, I passed my delegation report to the shadow cabinet and to MPs and MEPs with a long-term interest in the Middle East, together with thoughts developed regarding the best strategy for encouraging future progress. Having seen the situation first hand enabled me to discuss it with much greater conviction and confidence in my meetings with my own Jewish constituents in London East. Whilst not espousing a Zionist agenda, I absolutely defended the right of the state of Israel to exist and prosper. I also attempted to move their thoughts forward to the need to find a political settlement allowing peaceful coexistence between Israelis and Arabs.

I also enjoyed the opportunity to visit Australia and New Zealand in 1987 as a member of the official EP delegation. The range of subjects covered was breathtaking. I studied their labour law and equality policies; strategies to fight domestic violence; kangaroo culling and aboriginal rights. Prime Minister Bob Hawke was a charismatic figure whose government had succeeded in cementing a progressive social contract between both sides of industry. After consulting Australian women who put violence at the top of their list of priorities, the Labour government had conducted a serious campaign against domestic violence. I made firm friends with MP Helen Clarke who has since become Prime Minister of New Zealand. I trust her economic policies are less monetarist than New Zealand suffered in the eighties. David Lange was a robust and ebullient PM of New Zealand at the time, particularly in his policy of no nuclear vessels in the country's ports.

The British High Commissioner I remember was particularly patronising at an official dinner about our New Zealand friends. I recalled my Quaker background and thus implicitly my support for the government. Lord Plumb MEP promptly said how much he had always admired Quakers. Such diplomacy would stand him in good stead as President of the EP! I left in disgrace because I had dared to complain that the MEPs' wives had been excluded from the official dining room ! On my return I was able to explain Australian and New Zealand problems with the Common Agricultural Policy to the whole Parliament and to pass on other economic and social policy information to interested MEPs and MPs.

Second election victory

In 1987 Eva Eberhardt, a European feminist activist had joined our Ilford office as my women's officer. Thanks to Eva we were able to propose new equal opportunities policies at home and at EU level. Eva helped me to a greater understanding of equality policies and how to transform laws into reality. Sadly we would have to wait for a Labour government to enact laws on pro-rata rights for part-timers; parental leave; and better maternity protection. Strange for someone recruited for her social policy and equalities expertise Eva found herself organising a rock concert and party for the 1989 Election campaign. Barking Town Hall had seen nothing like it. Eva had managed to persuade Billy Bragg, Porky the Poet and talented local groups to perform for nothing. The town hall was packed with revellers from Barking and Dagenham enjoying good music and humour. It was with trepidation that I joined Billy Bragg on the platform to encourage people to vote Labour and for me at the forthcoming election. What effect it had I did not know, except that we doubled our majority to well over 25,000 votes. This was of course largely due to loyal local activists who campaigned at my side relentlessly in all weathers.

I was particularly thrilled to be joined in the EP by my friend and political soulmate Anita Pollack who achieved a wonderful victory in London South West with a majority of just 518 votes. She went on to be one of our most resolute environmental campaigners in the Parliament. One very pleasing outcome after the election was the election of Christine Crawley MEP as the dynamic Chair of the Women's Committee in the new Parliament who worked assiduously for EU laws on behalf of women. We spent many happy moments in that committee in a great spirit of sisterly friendship and cooperation. I appreciated also the ideas, hard work and solidarity of the newly elected Mel Read MEP who sat with me in the Economic and Monetary Affairs Committee 1989-1994.

Eva Eberhardt then went to Brussels to work for the European Commission. We moved together into a glorious loft-style flat in a disused factory. Her great companionship sustained me through the difficult campaigning battles of the nineties. We held many lively parties that allowed me to relax and really enjoy the company of my 'multinational' friends and colleagues.

Being deputy leader

I was proud to be elected Deputy Leader of the European Parliamentary Labour Party (EPLP) in the autumn of 1989. The leader at that time was Glyn Ford, and we got on very well, sharing many common ideas and values about the future of Europe. I remember very vividly being told by Neil Kinnock how pleased he was to see Glyn and me at the helm of the EPLP. Neil expressed the hope that we would increase liaison with the shadow cabinet and the Parliamentary Labour Party (PLP), and it fell to me to put into place a framework in order to achieve this. In 1989, one Labour MEP was appointed as a Liaison person for each committee. I would chair regular meetings where each Liaison MEP would flag up the current key issues, whether they were of grade A importance, grade B, and what was going to be controversial. I would communicate that back to the shadow cabinet, and to the PLP who'd also formed a liaison committee to meet with the EPLP. I would act as the link and try and iron out any policy differences. Liaison was not just with the shadow cabinet and the PLP, but with regional parties, with trade unions, with NGOs to a degree as well. It was an important and responsible job.

The post took me deeper into the British Labour Movement and into close relations with UK colleagues, and away from my European colleagues to a large degree. My committee work had to take a back seat. I missed work with continental colleagues.

In December 1992 my daughter Eleanore Christabel was born. I was overjoyed and embarked on a new life experience as a mother. I took 3 months off. With the help of the doughty and sisterly Mel Read MEP, the first woman quaestor in the EP, I was one of the first Parliamentarians to insist that they did not consider me off 'sick,' but rather on maternity leave. My colleague Kirsten Jensen, leader of the Danish Social Democrat delegation gave birth at the same time. We both found ourselves trying to balance being a mother with a demanding job. I decided that for Eleanore's sanity, she should not be dragged across Europe every week, so she stayed in England when I travelled. I trimmed my week a great deal in order to be here in the UK until Tuesday morning and back Thursday afternoon. My then husband was a considerable help and support. I was into very much a new era.

I was now a Parliamentarian with a family, and this increased the logistical complexity of the job. I was flying to Brussels three times a month, and once a month to Strasbourg. I was employing staff in three different places, in three different offices, ensuring that everybody knew what everybody else was doing. It was a demanding task. Computers, the internet and e-mail have revolutionised that dimension of work, but at the time faxes and phones were the only means of immediate communication. The travelling was very gruelling, and took a lot of energy. Most MEPs just wanted everything to be in Brussels, which would have been easier, but sadly it was not to be.

Meanwhile, liaison was improving all the time between the EPLP and the Labour movement and of course we played a great role in 1994 at the European Elections, having a massive victory with 62 members elected. That indicated a country ready to change the government at the next General Election. With so many MEPs we put a lot into the Labour movement in terms of supporting local activities, all with a European dimension. We also were able to talk in most constituencies to all the various groups there, and a lot of members really did work hard to get over a positive European message to schools and colleges. That was invariably our priority.

It was a joy to be joined by Glenys Kinnock MEP who brought great intellect and hard graft to bear on behalf of the developing world. Phillip Whitehead MEP, the distinguished documentary film maker, became a firm ally and friend. Also most welcome to the European Union were three new member states: Finland, Sweden and Austria, whose social democratic heritage greatly enriched our political and cultural debate.

Looking after the constituency

One of the major employers in my former constituency is the Ford Motor Company at Dagenham. After my re-election in 1989 I decided in the interest of my constituents to specialise in promoting the needs of the European car industry. I joined the Economic, Monetary and Industrial Affairs Committee and asked to be rapporteur on the future of the car industry in Europe, a proposal which my colleagues accepted. It was obvious Industrial Affairs Commissioner Martin Bangemann made policy over lunch with the big motor industry chiefs, a course which was neither democratic nor appropriate, nor indeed conducive to the long term success of the industry. A more democratic approach was called for, in which the Commission engaged with the views of the workforce, and fed them into policy-making as well.

Helping me in this work was my first ever Brussels assistant Hilary Lewison. She worked tirelessly on my behalf enabling me to develop car industry policy. Nothing was too much for her and she ensured I had reliable support when I was also elected Deputy Leader of the European Parliamentary Labour Party.

In my two reports on the car industry in the early nineties, I laid down the principle that management, workers and academic commentators should all have a say in EU industrial policy. This was an idea rarely practiced by the EU Commission at this time. To this end I suggested the formation of a permanent forum for each major industry, through which the Commission would consult with all the key players perhaps twice yearly, drawing upon the information it received to inform future policy. My report was overwhelmingly adopted by the European Parliament, winning support from colleagues of all parties and countries. I felt that I had won respect for tackling an unglamorous area of the economy where few women had dared to tread before.

Parallel to this, I set about giving these ideas actual implementation in the car industry. I contacted Dennis Gregory of Ruskin College, and Chris Firth from the Motor Industry Local Authority Network, and they became my unpaid and long-suffering advisors, whose expertise was absolutely invaluable. I met all significant management and trade union leaders in the European car industry. Through Dennis and Chris, I built up links with the Trade Unions, gradually convincing them to strengthen their European focus. Eventually I was able to set up the first ever European Car Forum, with all the key players (management; trades unions; academics; consumers; parliamentarians; civil servants) joining together for a two-day conference in Brussels. Midge Mackenzie, an independent film maker and also my friend, filmed the event for posterity, also giving me a wonderful visual aid when explaining my work to schools and other organisations.

My work on behalf of the car industry had three far-reaching consequences. Firstly, I believe it stimulated President Jacques Delors to create Objective Four of the European Social Fund. This is for the retraining of workers threatened with redundancy, principally from the car industry, but also from other economic sectors like textiles. Secondly, my work played a part in reinforcing British trade union views that they had a common cause with their colleagues in other countries, and helped to legitimise the expression of this conviction in a pan-European forum. This was a change which took place at every level, from shop-floor workers to figures such as Tony Woodley, the TGWU national officer for the car industry, and General Secretaries Roger Lyons (MSF), John Edmonds (GMB) and Bill Morris (TGWU). I stressed again and again that it was both right and absolutely necessary for the unions to engage fully with the European policy-making process, and that by doing so they could make a positive difference to the lives of their members. In addition, I began a campaign to persuade the Trade Union movement to implement this approach in a practical way by opening up offices in Brussels, to match those of the employers' representatives and the trade associations. In doing so, the seeds were sown for an important development in European civil society culminating in the situation today, in which we have a permanent TUC representative in Brussels, a GMB office and regular meetings of trade union officials with the Commission and with MEPs of all nationalities.

The third result of my work on the car industry concerned the allocation of roles between the Commission and the Parliament. In an important area of the economy, in which the Commission had previously taken unilateral decisions, the input of the Parliament and all key industry players was well respected. In effect we had asked 'Can we play too?' Now the EU institutions could not ignore the voice of civil society. Furthermore, the Parliament's ability to take initiatives that the Commission had to follow up on had been strengthened. Constitutionally, this was very significant, challenging the original allocation of functions where only the Commission had had the right of initiative. It gave the Parliament an enhanced voice and role, not just with respect to the car industry, but indeed in all areas of policy. Certain elements in the EU Commission were less than enthusiastic about this shift in the distribution of power between itself and the Parliament. However the Commission had little choice in the face of the Parliament's democratic mandate and the determination of many MEPs. Above all it represented an important and indispensable development of European civil society. This was badly needed to balance the weight of a few powerful industrial lobbies.

During the nineties I worked hard to convince the local authorities in my constituency that it was important for them to develop a proper European strategy. A lot of my energies went into convincing each of the authorities in London East to appoint a European officer responsible to the chief executive, and into encouraging them to acquaint themselves with the whole range of European funding which they could potentially win. To coordinate European funding bids and to share experience, I founded London East

European Forum with the local TEC - LETEC. This brought together all the key players in the region, and provided them with the opportunity to hear about some of the amazing training projects which Newham and other enterprising local authorities had been able to run with money awarded from the European Social Fund. These initiatives played a part in stimulating an influx of £150 million of European funding into my constituency between 1995-7. Another important factor in securing EU funding for London during the nineties was the institution of regular meetings of all the London Labour MEPs. In the absence of a London government, we realised that if we could lobby with one voice on behalf of London as a whole, we would provide a much more effective regional interface between the nation state and the European Union, and would enhance London's European profile. So indeed it proved, when we finally secured Objective 2 regional fund money for London, acting in coordination with London local authorities through the Association of London Government. This led to the development of serious infrastructure and job creation projects in some of the most deprived London Boroughs.

It was always tough explaining my job to the people of London East. One had to rely mainly on local radio and newspapers. The 1990s boom in local radio helped. New stations were desperate for material, and they always gave very fair coverage. I sought always to communicate a particular issue in a way that was understandable and meaningful, and which connected with people on the street. Take the directive on the protection of pregnant women in the workplace, for example. I decided that we should campaign using the slogan 'Bang the Drum for Mum.' My enterprising assistant Tessa Jones went to a local costumier and dressed up as a clown and we went around the streets of Ilford with a big drum. Needless to say such antics were not part of her contract. We handed out leaflets explaining how significant the directive was. People were amazed to learn how far behind the UK lagged in maternity provision. Our efforts paid off and we received extensive local press coverage.

I also organised a joint press conference on the same topic with Tony Blair and Kirsten Jensen, the leader of the Danish Social Democrats, when both she and I were pregnant in 1992. We set out to show the disparity between generous levels of maternity provision in Denmark and the meagre entitlements for British women. We achieved a paragraph in *The Times*, although amusingly it looked as though Tony Blair had fathered both children! Bringing Kirsten across from Denmark where conditions were better, vindicated my long-standing motto: 'Let all European citizens enjoy the best which exists.' If other countries can provide such a quality of life, why can't we? And if we have the best, as in the case of the BBC, why can't it be replicated elsewhere?

Similar campaigns were employed in the 1994 election which led us to a remarkable victory and a further doubling of our majority in London East !

1994 was to be a year of enormous changes in my Ilford and Brussels offices. Sadly Tessa Jones left us for new pastures. Sharon Spellar stepped in and soon became a most valued member of our team. Sharon's patience with constituents' complex problems and my incessant demands never ceased to amaze me. Louise Tinkler, who had taken over from Hilary Lewison and worked loyalty and diligently on my behalf in Brussels, was offered a new post. Natalie Wojtan, a dynamic multilingual woman joined our team in Brussels. We were kindred spirits. Her intellectual strengths were going to prove invaluable as we started arguably the most difficult political campaign in a very complex policy area.

Back in the Ilford office, we were joined by Paul Evans, my new political advisor who worked tirelessly on research for my speeches. Paul produced newsletters for the constituency which were essential in communicating our work to local people.

Television without frontiers

Following the 1994 election, I took my seat in the Committee for Culture, Media, Education and Sport, feeling that these policy areas had received insufficient attention from Labour members in the past.

Audio-visual policy was gaining in importance in the European Union at this time. In all EU countries, more than 60% of films shown on TV were American in provenance, rising to as much as 80% in some cases. This was partly a result of the development in the eighties of cable and satellite channels, through which the American audio-visual industry had greatly strengthened its position. At the same time, as is still the case today, it was almost impossible to view a film from another European country on TV before midnight. So we had a situation in which on the one hand the Americans were able to treat Europe as an extension of its own internal audio-visual market, whilst on the other EU TV and filmmakers were failing to achieve the same common market for their own programmes and films.

As a response to these pressures, the Commission had proposed the Television Without Frontiers Directive, adopted in 1989. This aimed to increase the circulation of TV programming and film within the EU, to strengthen the European audio-visual industry, and to assure cultural diversity in the face of increasing American market dominance. To this end, the Commission's proposal had stated that at least 51% of 'fiction' (drama, film and documentary) shown on TV screens in the EU must originate from EU member states. A strong battle was fought over the substance of the directive. As a result of extensive lobbying of Margaret Thatcher by Ronald Reagan, the then Conservative government secured a very damaging amendment to the original 1989 directive, which changed the original 51% obligation to say that this should apply 'wherever practicable.' The addition of these words in effect drove a coach and horses through the directive, allowing channels to evade the requirements of the directive on the

85

pretext that transmitting 51% of European material was not a commercially viable option.

In March 1995 the Commission proposed a new version of the Television Without Frontiers Directive, with the aim of strengthening it and also updating it to take account of developments over the 1989-1995 period, such as the emergence of teleshopping. The new version took out the words 'wherever practicable,' and also inserted a new and extremely enlightened provision which would require new channels, once they had been operating for three years, to invest at least 5% of their turnover in indigenous production. In making this addition, the Commission was following in the footsteps of the French and Canadian governments, who had imposed a legal obligation upon their broadcasters to invest between 10-20% of their turnover in French/European or Canadian production. The French and Canadian experience has been extremely positive in sustaining successful indigenous audio-visual industries, and continues to do so. The resulting investment of approximately £100 million per year in European film from a broadcaster such as Canal Plus clearly compares very favourably with, for example, BSkyB's £16 million film investment per year, and has played a major role in supporting the indigenous film industry across Europe. Moreover, such obligations are commercially viable, helping Canal Plus for example to build up its position as one of the most successful transfrontier media giants today. Just 5% of turnover invested in original production by the top 6 pay-TV operators would invest 300 million euros into our audio-visual industry!

The Chair of the Committee for Culture, Media, Education and Sport was Luciana Castellina, a great friend of mine and an icon of European Left politics. We worked closely together throughout the TV Without Frontiers campaign. At the first meeting of the socialist MEPs on the committee, I was honoured to be voted coordinator and spokesperson for the socialist group. This entailed responsibility for reconciling the different points of view within the socialist group, as well as defending our common position at meetings of all the political group coordinators. Opinion on the Television Without Frontiers Directive varied widely across our group, the Party of European Socialists. On the one hand, there were the Swedes, who wondered why we needed the directive at all, but who were very keen to incorporate an amendment to outlaw advertising on children's TV. On the other hand, my French, Belgian, Greek, Portuguese, and Italian colleagues were very much in favour of the Commission's proposals. The British Conservative government was content with the terms of the old directive and opposed any tightening of its provisions.

Despite this range of opinion, there was a very significant degree of cross-party cooperation and agreement within the Culture Committee in the European Parliament and beyond. After hours of detailed discussions, nearly all political groups supported the thrust of the Commission's proposals, the only exception being the Christian Democrats, under heavy pressure from media moguls Bertelsmann and Kirch in Germany. All the coordinators on the committee bar one were women, and all were very committed to developing a strong cultural dimension to the activities of the European Union. Together we led a drive to attempt to persuade the members of our individual political groups that the Commission's proposed changes were vital both for the future of the European audio-visual industry and in order to promote greater cultural partnership and diversity across Europe. I made speech after speech saying that the screen was one of two great curricula of the heart and the mind - the other being education - and that unless young people have the opportunity to view the streets of Mannheim, Madrid, Manchester and Módena as well as Miami and Manhattan, they can never be expected to develop any real understanding of their fellow Europeans, and hopefully one day empathise with them. In some ways we have had less European cultural exchange in the 1980s and 1990s than we did in the 1950s and 1960s, let alone over the longer course of our history.

The Committee cooperated very closely with the Commission, especially the responsible Directorate-General, DG 10. Two senior Commission officials, Gregory Paulger and Jean Michel Baer became close colleagues and friends during the long deliberations of the revised directive. The European Parliament and Commission worked as equal partners, in a way hardly seen before 1994, in part due to the use of the new co-decision procedure, and in part because of the presence of some very strong coordinators on the committee. We met regularly with Spanish Conservative Commissioner Oreja and with senior civil servants to discuss possible modifications to the original proposal. If the EP and the Commission could present a united front, we would be very strong in the face of any ministerial reluctance that we encountered in the Council.

The lobby for and against the directive

It was clear we wouldn't be successful in persuading certain governments of our case without pressure from below. I therefore set about forming a consortium of representatives from the UK audio-visual industry, encompassing BECTU (the Broadcasting Entertainment Cinematograph and Theatre Union); Equity (the actors' union); the Writers Guild; the National Musicians Union; the National Union of Journalists; the Directors' Guild; and the Producers' Alliance for Cinema and Television. All of them met with me regularly over the 1994-1999 period, and all were united behind the Commission's vision for the Television Without Frontiers Directive, recognising its importance for the future of their industry, and the investment that it would generate into original programme-making and skilled jobs for their members.

I was joined at this time by Midge Mackenzie, a distinguished independent film director who agreed to act as my media advisor. She worked tirelessly introducing me with generosity to key people in the UK audio-visual industry and advising on the best way for the new consortium to lobby for the revised directive. Her experience and creative imagination were of constant inspiration to me. When the lobbying against our position was very heavy, Midge helped keep me sane and robust.

I acted as a kind of channel for dialogue, transmitting information to the members of the consortium regarding legislative developments inside the EU institutions, whilst feeding back their concerns to the Parliament and Commission. We also discussed together how best to lobby the Commission and MEPs. It was decided the consortium would form a delegation to visit Brussels and speak to opinion formers directly about the Television Without Frontiers Directive.

There was colossal lobbying from American and some European media moguls, who focused their pressure on a number of my colleagues. The audio-visual industry was fast becoming America's biggest export industry, and the Motion Picture Association of America wanted nothing that would harm the penetration of US films, TV sitcoms and drama onto European screens. In this, it received the full backing of the American administration, as revealed in a leaked document from the American embassy in Paris at this time which showed that they were determined to do everything in their power to sabotage the directive and any further genuine strengthening of European audio-visual policy through broadcast and investment quotas. Their strategy was spelt out in black and white. Their aim was that the word 'culture' should never be mentioned in any discussions on the directive. They were also determined to try and split Europeans one from another. They were led by the powerful lobbyist Jack Valenti, Head of the Motion Picture Association of America.

In order to influence British members, I organised a big press conference with the TV consortium I've described, which took place in February 1996. With strategic intervention from Midge Mackenzie, we secured the attendance of a whole array of well-known individuals spanning the media and audio-visual community, including actors Bob Hoskins and Michael Cashman, directors Piers Haggard and Trix Worrell, and representatives from the BECTU trade union. Sadly only *The Daily Telegraph* covered the event, carrying a small article in which it quoted Bob Hoskins' comment: 'Television is our Hollywood; let us support it, not destroy it. That means supporting our creators, and investing money in creation.' Shortly after the press conference, the consortium took its lobby to the Parliament in Brussels. It was the first time that the creative community in Britain had done anything of this kind. Commission representatives were both very pleased and very surprised to see us. Director-General of the Culture DG, Colette Flesch, told me: 'We didn't think the British cared; now we know they do.'

In order to influence public opinion and the government and to air the issues in the Television Without Frontiers Directive, I and my staff organised a fringe meeting in a cinema during the 1997 Labour Party Conference in Brighton. We secured the premier of one of Bob Hoskyn's films 'Seven,' and free food for everyone. I convinced three culture ministers to appear on the same platform - Chris Smith MP, Italian Deputy Prime Minister Veltroni and former French Culture Minister Jack Lang. Veltroni even flew into Britain in the midst of a budget crisis forgetting his conference pass in the process. Security was tight and even such a distinguished guest was refused entry until a new pass was prepared. I chaired a packed meeting. There was unanimity among the speakers that some form of regulation promoting indigenous production on our television screens was necessary. The extent and nature of that varied with Veltroni and Lang in favour of strong broadcast and production quotas. David Puttnam approached me afterwards and suggested I might like to try film production as a career after such an impressive line-up!

It was hard to gain publicity in Britain for our campaign. For reasons which still remain unclear, both the BBC and ITV were reluctant to lend their support, or indeed say anything about the directive at all. I did, however, manage to persuade Michael Grade, the then chief executive of Channel 4, to launch *The Madness of King George* in Brussels, and to use the opportunity to give a speech on the directive. His position was that if quotas were needed in order to strengthen the audio-visual industry then they should be accepted, which amounted to an endorsement, albeit a reluctant one, of the Commission's proposals. Getting press coverage was also difficult. The story might have disappeared completely were it not for Polly Toynbee, to whom my colleague Phillip Whitehead MEP and I explained what was at stake. She understood the importance of the issues, and wrote two big articles. Needless to say certain newspapers with US television interests did not print a word on the issue.

A final lobby before the first reading vote in Spring 1996 was organised with prominent creators in the European Film industry, inter alia Wim Wenders, Claude LeLouche, John McGrath and Guiseppe Tornatore, all speaking at a packed Strasbourg press conference in favour of a stronger directive. John McGrath had always played a significant role in inspiring a strong and united campaign by British creators for greater investment in and broadcast of European programmes and films.

The legislative finale

The first reading of the revised Television Without Frontiers directive finally took place in Spring 1996. The co-decision procedure required an absolute majority of MEP's in support of the Commission's text and the amendments which we had put forward for any negotiation to take place with the Council of Ministers.

I spent many hours sitting with individual MEPs explaining the importance of the legislation and the positive economic and cultural impact which it would have. The

EPLP had to be convinced, too. Eminent documentary film maker, now Labour MEP Phillip Whitehead worked as a partner and ally in the campaign. At an EPLP meeting the week before the first reading Phillip presented the case for broadcast and investment quotas with gravitas. I called for a united Socialist Group position for reasonable amendments to strengthen our audio-visual industry and cultural diversity. Only+ a handful of EPLP colleagues were not convinced by our arguments.

German MEP Helmut Kuhne and Portuguese independent MEP Helena Vaz da Silva were also doughty campaigners throughout this protracted and tense struggle.

In the end, the result was very close, with a shortfall of roughly twenty votes below the 314 needed in order to keep the changes to the 1989 directive, which the Commission had proposed. We had lost a battle, but not lost the war.

Then came the second reading in Autumn 1996. On the day of the debate and vote I sat next to the charismatic Jack Lang, arguably the most famous former culture minister in Europe. We gave speeches, pleading with the Parliament to adopt by an absolute majority the removal of the words 'wherever practicable' and the addition of the provision concerning the investment of turnover in indigenous programme production. I remember our distress when we only garnered 292 votes, 22 fewer than we needed. Jack Lang was furious that some French MEPs had been missing from the vote, and gave an angry press conference questioning the co-decision requirement for an absolute majority of MEPs' votes irrespective of their actual presence in the chamber.

This disappointing result did not mean, however, that all was lost. Following the second reading in Parliament, the next stage was to go into face-to-face negotiations with ministers, as laid down by the co-decision procedure. We didn't succeed in persuading ministers to take out the words 'wherever practicable,' or the addition of the proposed investment clause. What we did achieve, however, was to secure the continued existence of the original 1989 directive, and to win some very valuable amendments. One of the most controversial changes which we as a committee secured was on sports rights, stating that each country must have autonomy to draw up a prescribed list of sports which must be shown free-to-air. The necessity of this became clear when we learnt that rights to the 2002 and 2006 World Cups had been bought by a pay-TV operator, with no guarantee that they would be sold on to free-to-air channels in Europe. We convinced the Commission of the need for an amendment, and they helped us draft it in such a way that it would work. Although the lobby against us was phenomenally active, we succeeded in incorporating it into the final version of the directive. Council of Ministers' objections to this new provision failed in the face of a united European Parliament position; a lesson being learnt across all parliamentary committees.

The directive in fact split the member states on an almost North-South basis. MEPs from Spain, Portugal, Italy, Greece, France and Belgium were all very much behind the Commission's proposals, whereas those from countries such as the Netherlands, UK, Germany and Scandinavia tended to be opposed or sceptical, partly due to the influence of the American lobby and the Motion Picture Association (MPA) of America in particular. The MPA's chief spokesman, Jack Valenti has proved himself to be, time and time again, arguably the most powerful lobbyist in the world. When I embarked on this campaign to strengthen European content on our screens and create more jobs in our TV/Film industries I had not realised what I would be up against. It was undoubtedly my first experience of 'high politics.' Many of us who came from Northern Europe felt that, had we received more support from our national parliaments and our domestic political parties, more could have been achieved. Nevertheless, I still consider the battle over the Television Without Frontiers directive to have been one of the most significant and important of the 1994-1999 period. Arguably, it was almost as contentious as economic and monetary union or any of the social legislation over that period. I still fervently believe that we must 'watch ourselves' more on TV if ever we are going to build greater understanding between European nations.

Toil and glamour in culture and media

Parallel to my activities on the Television Without Frontiers Directive, I was writing a report for the European Parliament on the Future of Public Service Broadcasting in the Digital Age. I was asked to fulfil this role following a decision taken by the coordinators in consultation with their political groups. They felt public service broadcasting was a topic of such importance that Parliament must itself take the initiative on it, rather than waiting for the Commission to act. In my report, I sought to underscore the place of public service broadcasting in a democratic society, arguing that it was part of the infrastructure of citizenship, and couldn't therefore be considered in the same category as commercial channels.

I made the proposal that there should be a special provision in the treaties of the European Union acknowledging the democratic, cultural and social significance of public service broadcasting within civil society, and establishing the autonomy of member states to decide on the mandate of their public service broadcasters, and whether they should be funded from public resources or otherwise. Midge Mackenzie worked closely with me on the report always ensuring the best use of our material. The report was a trend-setting document, and was heavily endorsed by public service broadcasters as a positive affirmation of what they were doing, and as a statement of how they should be developing in a digital age. Midge was keen we should win the maximum publicity for the report and she engineered a press conference with Luciana Castellina at the European Parliament office in Paris. Prominent figures from both the French media and press attended. My colleague and friend Jerome Clement, President of the Franco-German Cultural channel ARTE sat in the front row. He stood up to thank me and to emphasise that this was the first European report not only to defend but to actively promote public service broadcasting in the new digital age.

Following the adoption of my report by the Parliament in September 1996, we lobbied hard to secure a provision on public service broadcasting of the kind I had suggested, which was eventually achieved in the form of a special protocol to the Amsterdam Treaty. We owe a debt of thanks to the Dutch government for pushing the idea during its Presidency in 1997. In the initial stages of our campaign, however, we found our efforts frustrated due to concern in some quarters that a public service broadcasting provision would compromise the integrity of the competition articles of the treaties. The issue was partly solved through the positive intervention of the Irish Culture Minister, Michael D. Higgins. He made it a priority of the Irish Presidency during the second half of 1996 to obtain agreement for the protocol, highlighting the contribution of public service broadcasting to society, immortalised in the words 'The EU cannot live by commercialism alone.' So the governments finally put their signatures to the protocol. Clearly they also believed that the EU was about more than simply regulating carrots and cars!

Despite this victory, the tension between the competition articles of the Union and the role of public service broadcasting remains. It will continue to do so until there is greater clarification in the treaties as to what constitutes citizenship, and the rights associated with it. Thus, if I were writing the Charter of Fundamental Rights for the European Union, there would be an important passage enshrining not only the freedom of speech, but also the right to media pluralism, to public service broadcasting, and to universal access to the means of communication. At present, we still have the completely unacceptable situation in which Commission civil servants working on competition matters are making judgements as to whether public service broadcasters should be permitted to launch thematic channels. Public service channels commission, produce and broadcast a much higher percentage of home grown programmes than commercial channels. Channelling more investment into public service broadcasting and its new digital channels is absolutely vital if we are to succeed in retaining our cultural autonomy and self-esteem in the face of the ever-increasing globalisation of culture.

In addition to my role as coordinator, and my work writing the report on public service broadcasting, I took on two additional responsibilities. Firstly, I accepted the Presidency of a group called Cities and Cinemas, a local authority network designed to support best practice on how to support local cinema and the showing of world film across Europe. I thus received even more invitations to speak at meetings all over Europe.

Secondly, I was elected in 1997 as president of the European Parliament Cinema and Audio-visual Intergroup. The intergroup organised discussions on key issues, and we would invite high profile guest speakers. The competition Directorate-General, DG4, decided that it wanted to draw up guidelines for public service broadcasting, suggesting that public service broadcasters should only carry programmes not covered by commercial channels. This potentially could have meant the Brussels competition authorities deciding the BBC could only do opera but not *Top of the Pops*. The Competition Commissioner, Karel van Miert and the Secretary General of the European Broadcasters Union were invited to speak in open debate. We had a packed meeting with a large media presence and it undoubtedly contributed to the subsequent dropping of the proposal. I felt proud to have prevented a particularly narrow-minded section of the EU Commission from dictating the nature of our public service broadcasting.

Following Labour's election in 1997 it was decided that, in order to improve cooperation between the EPLP and the Government, in each subject area there should be an MEP responsible for liaison with the appropriate minister. I was nominated as Link Person by Tony Blair with the Ministers in the Department of Culture, Media and Sport. The stakes were very high and one had to be highly professional. I was required to deliver detailed and reliable information to the Secretary of State and other Ministers. It was an honour to have such a responsible role and to be able to make a contribution to the new Labour government.

During the UK presidency in the first half of 1998, I produced over twenty briefings for ministers, highlighting the issues that they would face when chairing meetings, and including information not supplied by their civil servants. I organised a big social event in my flat in Brussels for Mark Fisher, the former Arts Minister, to which I invited prominent figures from the cultural community in Belgium. I can remember watching Nana Mouskouri, then an MEP, using the occasion to lobby Mark for the return of the Elgin Marbles - an opportunity that no self-respecting Greek parliamentarian would miss.

A new member of staff joined us at this time in Brussels. Rebecca Willis worked with us as a researcher. I am grateful for her calmness and intellectual rigour.

All my different responsibilities combined to form a heavy but interesting workload, and one which was often immensely enjoyable.

I attended the Cannes Film Festival a number of times. It felt like an annual reward and treat for my hard and often invisible work. It had always been tough getting coverage of our work in the British media. In addition to being a very pleasurable few days, it provided a golden opportunity to talk to many influential people in the industry about the work we were doing in the EU to strengthen the European film industry. I also learnt a great deal about the film industry from them.

I remember a number of film premières at which the actual protagonists from the film came and sat down in the next row of seats: Fanny Ardant and Jean Rochefort; Sean Penn ; John Travolta and Emma Thompson to name but a few! I also had the privilege of seeing all of the most significant European films for the coming year, many of which - *Secrets and Lies, Breaking the Waves* and *Eight and a Half Days* - went on to critical acclaim.

On one memorable night I remember equipping Natalie Wojtan and Lucy (from Phillip Whitehead MEP's office) with my own dresses to attend a gala evening. After a rapid phone call to my great friend John McGrath I also succeeded in borrowing a dinner suit for Phillip Whitehead so we could all enjoy the evening together. We really had earned such a treat after all the campaigning over Television Without Frontiers.

At one lunch in Cannes I sat next to French director Claude Lelouch who talked about his five children and how he gave them all a video camera 'ensuring they would never view the world the same again.'

The Mayor of Strasbourg, Catherine Trautmann, (also a long standing colleague and friend), had become Lionel Jospin's Culture Minister in the late 1990s. She kindly invited Luciana Castellina and me to the opening night of the 1998 festival. Rebecca came too. Dressed in our best togs we waited downstairs in the Hotel Majestic for Catherine to arrive. The jury led by Martin Scorsese passed by. He was as short as Sigourney Weaver was tall. Inexplicably she waved to me. I smiled back. UN Secretary-General Kofi Annan was introduced to us all. A mild-mannered and gracious man. The theme that year was cinema's contribution to human rights. It was a glorious evening culminating in a sumptuous dinner surrounded by various stars. I chose my moment and congratulated Sabine d'Azema for her performance in 'On Connait Ma Chanson' which was dedicated to the memory of Denis Potter. She was thrilled that someone in Britain had seen the film and recognised the honour the director Alain Resnais had paid Potter.

Other campaigns, as on copyright protection led to my meeting other great stars and personalities: Jean-Michel Jarre, Claudia Cardinale and the Corrs to name but a few.

Jean Michel Jarre spoke with great fluency and aplomb about creator's rights. Their presence certainly helped to convince most MEPs that copyright must protect creators' livelihoods. Meeting Dario Fo in a Strasbourg lift inspired the best Italian I have ever spoken. How could one possibly not speak to such a great writer and artist. He had come to Strasbourg to campaign against the patenting of genes. What else?!

As someone for whom music has always been a central part of my life, I particularly treasure memories of time spent with the great Yehudi Menuhin. Our committee worked to ensure that the Menuhin Foundation received funds from the EU for its invaluable work on behalf of disadvantaged children in inner cities. Lord Menuhin was the most gracious, refined and dignified person I have ever met. I had the great pleasure to accompany him to a school in a poor quarter of Brussels where he showed how music, mime and dance could help immigrant children come to terms with their new environment. I shall never forget the young children miming playing the violin with the great Maestro. He came often to our Committee and was always seeking an innovative way to secure greater understanding between cultures. It was a joy to have watched and listened to his words of wisdom, not to mention his magnificent violin playing.

Another musical memory will always stay with me. After a magnificent concert by the European Union Youth Orchestra, (organised by the indefatigable Joy Bryer), I met and heard recollections from Vladimir Ashkenazy. I could hardly believe I was sitting next to one of my musical heroes whose playing of Rachmaninov in particular had so inspired me to practice the piano as a teenager. He even admitted he needed some urging as a youngster to practice. I found him charming and modest. He spoke mainly of his work encouraging and supporting young musicians.

Further insiprational cultural delights were found on the various language courses I attended. Visiting Girona for a Spanish course with Luciana Castellina and our two mothers we spent a glorious evening at the opening of the Perelada festival. Jose Carreras and Montserrat Caballe sang for the villagers who had crowded into the main square. The warmth, joy and pride shone on everyone's faces. I was so moved that these two great Catalan singers were celebrating with the people of their own region to thank them for enduring a large festival in their small village. I felt honoured to meet both singers. Jose Carreras captivated me with his demure grace and charm. I was in awe of his courage returning to the stage after a life threatening illness. Montserrat Caballe was serene with a hint of haughtiness - surely allowed in a diva!

After the hard fought campaigns for cultural diversity on the screen, Natalie Wojtan and Rebecca Willis sadly moved on to fresh pastures in the late nineties. I felt bereft. We had gone through so much together. Gwenda Jeffries Jones and Ben Wallis then took up the reins with great confidence in my Brussels office.

They too were loyal, intelligent and supportive, ensuring our campaigns for cultural diversity went from strength to strength. Throughout my tenure as Coordinator for the Socialist Group on Culture, Media, Youth and Sport I had had the pleasure of working with staff member Doriano Dragoni. His Italian diplomatic skills, humour and charm had always helped ensure we won key points and votes. I am indebted to him for his great support and loyalty.

Labour in power

And then of course came the long-awaited great Labour victory of May 1997. I remember being with my then husband as he was elected MP for Gravesham. Simultaneously I celebrated nine Labour victories in my own Euro constituency. I screamed with joy as my home constituency of Upminster went Labour. I was only sad my mother and stepfather were not alive to enjoy having a Labour MP. The celebrations passed me almost in a blur. I spent most of the early hours of the next morning giving interviews in French to Belgian and French radio and television stations. The day after the election I gave a commentary on the *France 3* evening news, which had to be timed down to the last second.

There was a great feeling of relief right across Europe that Labour had won and after 18 years the Tories were out. I remember returning to the Parliament after the victory and being hugged by people of all political complexions (with the exception of the far right). Colleagues were relieved that a very eurosceptic Conservative Party had gone after so long, and they welcomed the promise of a new era, of a new constructive engagement by Britain with them all. A different climate took hold overnight. It was quite wonderful. Suddenly we were welcoming ministers from our own political family to Brussels.

We then were quickly launched into the British Presidency in the first half of 1998. Labour MEPs played an absolutely critical role in briefing ministers, and accompanying them when they came to Brussels. There were so many of them coming and going, we could hardly keep track. You couldn't get into a lift in the European Parliament without meeting yet another British Labour minister! What a joy after the long dark eurosceptic years of Prime Ministers Thatcher and Major!

Many ministers had much experience of European affairs. Some, of course, like John Prescott, Richard Caborn or Joyce Quin had been Members of the European Parliament. We enjoyed a privileged relationship with such ministers. They of course had great influence on their colleagues. There were some that had less knowledge; but they were all very open and very grateful for our input. It didn't mean we didn't have difficulties, with British civil servants giving advice in one direction which some of us at times believed somewhat politically unhelpful. We felt that we as MEPs had a better understanding of the mosaic and tapestry of European politics. Sometimes one found oneself saying 'I really don't think it is a good idea to go down this road, Minister. We could be outvoted as it's qualified majority voting.'

Having Labour in power at home was very different from the previous 13 years. We had to have due regard to the policy aims Labour Government. Sometimes we were encouraged to vote by the government in the European Parliament on the future of the European Union against our own views and that of the PES group. We had interesting and heated discussions in the EPLP about future constitutional arrangements. The vast majority of Labour MEPs wanted the Parliament to have much more power, and the Labour Government wanted only a limited extension of qualified majority voting. Foreign and Home Affairs were difficult areas in which to convince governments to include us as equal partners in the decision making process. We had to sit down and find compromises. For the first time we were faced with the political reality of our own party in power. Meeting that challenge demanded one raised the level of one's political professionalism.

We also had by this time an annual Labour European conference, which was an important innovation, a recognition that you needed a special Labour Party conference on European affairs for party activists. I remember one of my delights was not only attending one of these conferences and speaking at workshops, informing Labour Party members of what we were doing, but actually getting Eddie Izzard to agree to come and do a meeting at the Labour Party Europe conference in Bexhill in 1997. I couldn't quite believe that Eddie found time to do it. With great humour he convinced 150-200 people at the end of the conference why he felt that Britain should embrace the rest of Europe very positively, and 'stop behaving like the tin cans tied on the back of the wedding car that you are longing to cut off when you reach the first corner.' He reminded people of our chequered and rather interesting European history and of how our language and identity has developed from many different cultural roots. He did this with great humour, aplomb and panache. I only wish that the rest of the population had had access to his hilarious and inspirational performance that day in his home town of Bexhill.

Twenty year retrospect

It has been a great privilege to have witnessed and been part of the European Parliament initially as an official and then for three terms as an MEP. Sadly the low turnout at the 1999 Euro election coupled with the new PR system led to the loss of my seat at this election. There is a lot I deeply miss: my former constituency; local Labour Party friends; European colleagues and European politics.

I have thus seen this imaginative and important institution develop and grow in stature and importance over 20 years. John Hume has rightly said that it is the embodiment of a very important value, that of 'humanity cooperating across frontiers.' In the Parliament one finds a cross section of humanity both in the broad selection of MEPs but also in the way they work together across frontiers.

When I first worked in the Parliament it was a body merely consulted by the Council of Ministers, but after the 1986 Single European Act it gained real powers of co-decision. The other institutions sat up and took notice. Always at the head of the Parliament has been a dedicated nucleus of parliamentarians absolutely committed to devising good quality legislation for Europeans and also to enhancing the European Parliament's importance. Staff members such as the present Secretary General of the EP, Julian Priestley, have also played a key role in this respect. Over time the European Parliament has won considerable powers of co-decision and thus greater democratic input on behalf of the people of Europe.

Attitudes towards the Parliament have changed as well. The European Commission now regards the EP as more of an equal partner and greater mutual respect now exists between the EU institutions. Ministers actually understand that MEPs are engaged in valuable work, and that they are not trying to snatch away their sovereignty without due cause. The press corps in Brussels has increased to become possibly the biggest in the world, or the second biggest after

Washington, and thus over time every newspaper has felt obliged to have its correspondent there to cover stories in some detail. Jacques Delors' prophecy that between 60% and 80% of social and economic legislation would be European in origin is a reality. The Labour government brought many progressive social laws onto the British statute book: parental leave; pro-rata rights for part-time workers; better employee rights in discrimination cases; and European works councils to name but a few. All originated at European level and were invariably inspired by the European Parliament.

The European Parliament has also flexed its 'own initiative' muscles in deciding to set up official enquiries on drugs; combating fraud; the scourge of BSE; and on racism and xenophobia. This latter action concluded in a formal declaration between the Presidents of the three institutions and the setting up of an Observatory on Racism in Vienna. Whether it has been a question of taking lead out of petrol; regulating food safety; protecting the environment or the creation of an observatory monitoring racism in Europe, the Parliament has brought a great, and generally positive influence to bear on the process of European integration. Parliamentarians now, provided they are diligent and professional, are gaining respect all the time, and are increasingly regarded as fundamental in terms of bringing a necessary democratic voice to the European Union. Where the Parliament has been firm and united in the co-decision procedure, it has been immensely powerful in ensuring its amendments are included in final legislation. This has begun to overcome the once justifiable complaint of decisions being made behind closed doors in smoke-filled rooms in the Commission and Council.

Where the European Parliament has defended the primacy of the general public interest and its expression in the development of European civil society it deserves well-earned praise. Landmarks in this included the Parliament opening up its doors to hold a Youth Parliament and a Pensioners' Parliament. They were great events, which brought ordinary people together across frontiers - the only way forward to build mutual and long-lasting peace and understanding. This is the only basis for further European integration.

Looking forward

With enlargement to include a further ten or more states there has to be an inevitable rationalisation in the membership of all the institutions. This will be tough in itself. There is also an economic reality, which will demand that the European Union spends more money to cope with the new enlargement. That is one of the enormous challenges that governments have to get to grips with. The budget for enlargement, with the need to embrace millions of poor Polish farmers, for instance, must reflect economic realpolitik on the part of national ministers. A significant reform of the Common Agricultural Policy cannot be ducked. The present policy cannot continue in its present form and cope with the enlargement envisaged. Also, the current budget of well under 2% of Community GDP is inadequate in an economic and monetary union. Numerous eminent European economists, as well as great European statespeople from Jacques Delors to Helmut Schmidt have urged national finance ministers to bite the bullet on this. The EU budget must be increased and be used to iron out inequalities between rich and poor regions, which could be aggravated through the adoption of the single currency.

One would hope to see expenditure on research and development and industrial policy increasing to ensure that Europe's key industries, including the media and cultural industries, can continue to excel, to blossom and deliver programmes to the rest of the world, as well as to bring indigenous creative production to our citizens.

The Parliament must enjoy co-decision in all areas of policy. It is not acceptable that Home Affairs are only subject to an opinion from Parliament. MEPs should be able to have some clear legislative say here. The same applies to foreign and security policy. Qualified majority voting should apply to all areas if European democracy is to earn its name. For example, the cultural sphere should no longer be a policy area requiring unanimous voting by ministers. I do appreciate why governments wish to retain unanimous voting for treaty changes, taxation and social security. That may change over time as the internal market becomes seriously distorted by wildly differing tax policies, for example. There will have to be a rapprochement of taxation levels, I would imagine, over time.

On the logistical side, I am a great defender of cultural and linguistic diversity. There will come a moment however, when although everyone will continue to be able to speak their own language, EU documents and indeed simultaneous translation may only be delivered in five or six languages. It is hard to envisage how else the ever-expanding Union will cope. And that will be one of the most difficult decisions to be taken, given the intrinsic link between language and cultural identity. The Parliament has its new building in Strasbourg as well as the one in Brussels. How long can this split site arrangement continue? Going to Strasbourg each month is like being the last carriage in a runaway express train shunted up a siding. For the Parliament to have more powers, to work effectively, to call the Commission and Council to account, and to do the job it clearly wants to do on behalf of European citizens, its location on one site is imperative.

These are the most thorny questions. Tackling them will take courage and foresight on the part of Europe's leaders. With a strong European Parliament urging them on, I am sure they will rise to the challenge.

Above all Europe's leaders must make a reality of European citizenship. They must overcome their fear of loss of sovereignty in areas such as education and appreciate that the EU can offer important added value. A very important cornerstone of the people's Europe has been the Socrates programme, designed to enable young people from primary schools through to university to join in exchanges

106

and projects with children and young people in other countries. There was never a dissenting voice in the Parliament about the vitality of this programme and its need for more money. We secured more resources year on year, and were able to open up the programme to increasing numbers of children and young people. There is still a long way to go. If Europe really is to be their economic, cultural and social oyster, then educational exchange programmes can help them make their way as true European citizens. More resources are still needed. One hopes EU priorities will shift over time as ministers understand the importance of underpinning European cooperation by European understanding between citizens in the different countries of the Union.

At nation state level, the BBC should launch a children's channel with European windows from other European broadcasters. The Franco-German cultural channel ARTE should have a partner here in Britain and offer a wider range of film and documentary from across Europe and the world. The Federal Trust has developed curriculum materials on European citizenship. Every young person should have access to them and be able to prepare for adult life as a European citizen with the knowledge and understanding of other cultures that that demands.

The two most powerful curricula of the mind come to us from the screen and school. There must be a greater European dimension in both if future generations are ever to feel the same empathy for fellow Europeans as they do for their own compatriots. Only that way lies long-lasting peace and prosperity.

The European debate in Britain must focus on why we are engaged in common political, economic and cultural endeavour with other Europeans. Our government and other opinion formers must reassert with confidence our belief in values that we share with fellow Europeans.

What we were engaged in as MEPs was exciting and fulfilling, producing tangible results for European citizens.

Sadly there was often active media disinterest in our work, making it hard to reach our constituents with news of our endeavours on their behalf. This was in large part due to the reluctance of part of the British media to engage with us and to recognise the positive features of European policies. This was evidenced by the very low turnout at the 1999 European elections.

Our societies are anchored in a strong welfare state of mutual solidarity among citizens, a common cultural heritage, industrial democracy, equality of opportunity, sustainable development and equal citizenship as expressed (inter alia) in universal access to high quality public service broadcasting. The government must move public opinion behind a pro-European social democratic agenda.

The citizens of Europe expect no less from their British partners.

Fifteen Years in a Growing Parliament
The development of the membership and powers of the European Parliament

Florus Wijsenbeek

Introduction

Jean Monnet was born and bred in brandy. He was born in 1888 in Cognac into a family of traders in the distilled product of a grape unsuitable to turn into good wine and thus used for other purposes: the Pineau de Charentes. That the 'House of Monnet' is now owned by the German firm 'Asbach Uralt,' producers of, in my opinion, a brandy of definitely lesser quality than the French variety, might be called one of the effects of the European unification process. This firm has in turn recently been taken over by the Dutch distillers, Bols, where my first boss on the path to European politics, the former Secretary of State for European Affairs, Hans de Koster, was once President of the Board.

Monnet's route into politics, although not directly relevant to this study, is characteristic of the origins of the European Union, the goal of which - the avoidance of war between the states of Europe - is no longer first and foremost in the minds of the current generation of politicians. During the First World War the export of cognac to the United States and Great Britain was severely hampered by the requisitioning of shipping by the French Government to transport weapons and troops. Nobody in the Government, in exile in Bordeaux far away from threatened Paris, thought about the organisation of return freight. But Jean Monnet, who though young, had already travelled to America and England, proposed the pooling of resources and common organisation among the Allies to share loading capacity. He went to see Prime Minister Viviani, who agreed to the plan and charged him with organising it. From this point on Monnet continued to work in international cooperation, including a spell as assistant secretary general of the League of Nations. He also returned for a brief period to the cognac trade when the family firm needed sorting out during a difficult period.

I stress Jean Monnet's commercial background in order to frame an incident related to me by some of the early civil servants. At the very beginning of the European Coal and Steel Community (ECSC) Common Assembly, as the European Parliament was then called, when relations between the President of the High Authority and the Assembly became rather strained, Jean Monnet, as a company man, saw the relationship between the High Authority, the Council and the Assembly as comparable to those between the management, the board and the shareholders in a firm. In Cognac he would have called a shareholders' meeting at most once a year, in order to wine and dine them and inform them of the state of affairs. No questions were expected to be tabled, there being at most some measure of private after-dinner discussion. Not so with the members of the Common Assembly. They displayed in Monnet's eyes the insolence of tabling critical questions. After a first encounter he refused to confront them again. It needed all the powers of persuasion of his close associate, Etienne Hirsch, over several months before he would concede that it was natural for members of Parliament to put questions and that as President of the High Authority he had to answer them. Interesting as this story might be, others who knew Monnet well, such as the first secretary general of the ECSC, Edmond Wellenstein, with whom I have had a long discussion about his term of office, deny it and state, as would be more probable, that Monnet was on the contrary very much in favour of the Common Assembly as a counterpart to the power of the Council of Ministers.

This incident, if it ever happened, was by no means the only stumbling block on the path to the development of fully fledged democratic control by the representatives of the electorate at large. The first direct election took place in 1979, but it took another twenty years until the political supremacy of the elected body over the nominated Commission was confirmed with the resignation of the Commission under threat of censure by the Parliament in January 1999. The Parliament's legislative powers have been enhanced through the extension of the co-decision procedure, most recently at the Treaty of Amsterdam, which came into force in May 1999. But there are still, from an idealist's viewpoint, many inconsistencies and imperfections, the resolution of which depends on future generations of MEPs.

Personal involvement

I come from a family which is both very Dutch and very international and which has long been involved in trade and public affairs. On both my paternal and maternal sides, the family home was in a small town called Culemborg, in the midst of the countryside in the province of Gelderland, on the banks of the river Rhine. My great-grandfather Wijsenbeek owned a textile firm, a butcher's shop and a cigar factory. He was elected to the town council at the end of the nineteenth century and served as an alderman, which at the time was quite an achievement for a Jew. At a certain point he realised that producing one's own textiles was not very advantageous, and from then on he ordered his products from a cousin in Manchester to where he travelled often. My other great grandfather traded in wheat and owned a gin distillery. He was what could be called landed gentry and the family had its own pew in the local Dutch Reformed Church. The two great-grandfathers knew one another well and between them traded in virtually everything. Socially, however, the two families did not mix, segregated along religious lines as Dutch society still was, until my parents married in 1937.

My father, having read law at Leyden University and art history at Utrecht, settled in The Hague to become director of the municipal Fine Arts Service. He was also politically active, as his family had always been, in the Liberal Party. This brought many politicians and artists to our house, both from the Netherlands and abroad, and confronted me at an early age with discussions about the two internationally oriented occupations of art and politics.

During my high school years, at the elite school 'Het Nederlandsch Lyceum,' where the children of many politicians, senior civil servants and diplomats were educated, I ventured into politics and subscribed to the 'Jongeren Europese Beweging,' a branch of the Young European Federalists (JEF). In my final history examinations in 1963 I was questioned on the European integration process, something commented upon somewhat critically by the State Delegate present as 'All these new ventures which youth is engaged in these days.'

As a law and political science student at Leyden University I continued in this direction by taking European Law as one of my subjects and ventured into politics more seriously, being elected to the National Student Council, becoming president of the Liberal Student Organisation and serving on the board of the Leyden branch of the People's Party for Freedom and Democracy (VVD).

After graduation, and whilst reading political science in the USA, I received a letter from our party's Minister for European Affairs, the very wealthy grain merchant, Hans

De Koster, asking if I would come back and serve as his assistant, to organise the next electoral campaign in which he was to stand for the VVD as the number two on the list. This brought me right into the centre of European politics, sitting in a small office situated between that of the Minister of Foreign Affairs, Joseph Luns and that of De Koster. The two shared 'facilities,' the entrance to which was through my office. Luns frequently had to visit these and would question me on the way about what I was doing. On my reply 'Politics,' he would counter 'Behind this desk it should rather be diplomacy.' This is an occupation that has never attracted me, and that's a decision my wife fully agrees with.

When De Koster was promoted after the elections to become the Minister of Defence he invited me to accompany him, but I wanted instead to join the European Community. He first sent me to Luxembourg to go and see his cousin by marriage, Hans Nord, who was Secretary General of the Parliament. At the time, however, there was no post for a Dutchman available. De Koster then took the phone and called the Dutch Commissioner for Agriculture, Dr Sicco Mansholt, and within a short time I was seconded to the Commission's Legal Service in the Berlaymont building in Brussels. My specific job was to be secretary to the Vedel Committee that was to give advice to the Commission on institutional change. It was a tremendous opportunity to become acquainted with Europe. In addition to Georges Vedel there were some other formidable members: Jos Kapteyn for the Netherlands, now at the Court in Luxembourg, John Mitchell from Edinburgh University for the UK, and for Ireland Mary Robinson, later to become President of the Republic. My Head of Division was Claus Dieter Ehlermann, later to become Head of the Commission's legal service, but I had to submit my reports to Jacques Amphoux first, who would almost faint at their shortness and my scant respect for decorum. It was unacceptable to him if I wrote simply 'The meeting was called to order,' as he wanted instead 'The doyen Vedel did us the immense honour of being willing to open the meeting.'

In Brussels I shared an office with two other young new arrivals, Günther Burckhardt, now Director General for External Relations and a certain Del Prete, the nephew of Franco Maria Malfatti, the President of the Commission. We didn't see that much of this Del Prete in what was already too small an office; he would turn up once in a while at eleven in the morning, telling us how tired he was and would leave soon afterwards again to catch up on sleep or restart partying. He broke the unprecedented news to us, however, that his uncle would leave the Commission and return to Italy to become a cabinet minister. This was an interesting piece of information to take along when I moved from the Commission to the Parliament. The work of the Vedel committee being finished, I had been proposed for a post in the administration of the Customs Union, but in the meantime the party had sent me another letter, this time from the party president Haya van Someren-Downer. I had to report immediately to Luxembourg since they believed that one of theirs was to become the President of the Parliament and someone from the party had to be alongside to report what was going on. The VVD had very much stuck to the idea that the European Parliament was a place to send people who they would rather not keep at home.

Thus in early 1972 I moved to Luxembourg to become Chef de Cabinet to the future President, Dr Cornelis Berkhouwer. I was temporarily seconded to the Liberal group staff. The Secretary-General of the Group at the time, Louis Maury, was one of the most peculiar characters I have ever met. A tiny little man, always a bit crumpled and greasy, with bicycle clips on his trousers, he never did any serious work (that was reserved for myself and my friend and colleague Massimo Silvestro), but was known not only across the whole staff of about six hundred but throughout France, as he had in the early days of television won the brains and beauty contest 'La Tête et les Jambes.' Having acquired this fame and being a hero of the Resistance, he put himself up as a rival candidate against our group member, the Prince de Broglie, who did not really appreciate the gesture. Threatening that he would divulge Maury's peccadilloes with his pupils in the Lycée des Jeunes Filles in their common home town of Evreux if he refused, he offered Maury the post of Secretary General of the group in Luxembourg. This arrangement suited them both.

Louis Maury was constantly writing a book that would outdo all other books, but never seemed to progress beyond the 'Table of Contents.' Then one day he took us by surprise by announcing that he had finished it. He went to see the then Director General of Session Services and Printing and subsequent Secretary General, Hans Joachim Opitz, and asked permission to have his book printed in the Parliament printing shop. Opitz, who had heard the story about the book, did not believe that Maury could really have written anything of any length, and readily gave his permission. The next session there were no documents available, since the entire stock of paper had been used for Louis Maury's book. Additionally Maury helped to wreck the career of another colleague, the Group President at the time, the young French Deputy Jean Durieux, who was later to adhere to Le Pen. He added his name as co-author on the cover of the book, the title of which was 'Where President Giscard d'Estaing is wrong.' Durieux, a rising star who was very proud to have been invited to the presidential shoot at Rambouillet that very weekend, never made it beyond the gate. The security service had instructions to kick him out of the park on arrival and he never recovered his political career.

Berkhouwer, Durieux's predecessor as President of the Liberal Group, had in the meantime become President of the Parliament, and I had moved up with him. It was quite something for a twenty-eight year old. In those days of the double mandate the President had to divide his time between his home country and his European duties, and so the Chef de Cabinet had to serve as his permanent eyes and ears within the administration, often in his absence. Nothing of importance was decided without the Chef de Cabinet submitting it to the President. I received tremendous help

115

in this role from the Secretary General of the Parliament, Hans Nord. Hans was not only a compatriot and fellow Liberal, but we shared a lot more, having been to the same schools, belonging to the same clubs, and being bridge partners. We were friends right up until his untimely death in 1996, when I had the honour of speaking at his memorial service, as I did for Cornelis Berkhouwer, who died a few years before, in 1992.

Berkhouwer was the prototype of a constituency man. In the area from which he came, the agricultural region north of Amsterdam he was known as 'Boeren Keessie' (Farmers' Favourite). Everybody knew him and he knew everyone, if only from his frequent visits to all the pubs in the locality. Each election he scored more personal votes, even when the party as such occasionally lost. He had been a protégé of the party's founder, Professor Oud, who then came from the same region and personally selected the promising young solicitor, who presided over the Liberal representatives on Alkmaar local council, to become an MP in 1956. Berkhouwer was a member of the European Parliament from 1963, and succeeded René Pleven as President of the group from 1969 until his election to the Presidency in 1973. He remained a Vice President and member till 1984, when he ended his career sadly, having been accused of pinching a bottle of wine. This was typically Berkhouwer. He went around Europe exchanging all kinds of local specialities, starting out from home with a cheese, moving through wine or pâté and coming back bearing antique furniture, of which he had quite a collection in his converted farmhouse.

My job with him was not all that easy. When he was in the chair presiding over the plenary session of Parliament, I had to sit next to him, steering him through the procedures, and often he would turn around and make comments about others or me with the microphone on, which would draw either laughter or commiseration from everyone who understood Dutch. After Berkhouwer's Presidency, which I frequently had to defend discreetly against attempts to unseat him, I was asked to lead the Secretariat of the newly founded Federation of Liberal and Democratic Parties (ELDR). There I served under Gaston Thorn and subsequently under Willy de Clerq, doubling at the same time as group staff member for legal affairs.

I stood in the first direct elections in 1979, but narrowly missed making it into the top four on our party list. My position during those years was a bit peculiar because if any of the four Dutch liberals elected had vacated their seat, I would have stepped in. It made them very wary of crossing the street in my company!

Simone Veil, subsequently President of the Parliament, the Legal Affairs Committee and of the Group, did not appreciate my services highly and frequently shouted at me in public. Ironically, my distance from her made my work negotiating with other groups a lot easier. But when I was finally elected in 1984, we got along extremely well, after an initial showdown in which she acknowledged my change of status from member of staff to elected Member of Parliament.

Origins: From common assembly to Parliament

The earliest forms of European cooperation in the post war era were the Brussels Pact, predecessor to the WEU, and the Organisation for Economic Cooperation and Development (OECD), then called the Organisation for European Economic Cooperation (OEEC). The former was intended to assure mutual military assistance between the United Kingdom, France and the Benelux countries. The latter was designed to administer Marshall aid and included Germany, against whom the Brussels Pact was intended to protect its member states.

Many idealists in the federal movement, which existed before the war in the Pan-European Union founded by the

Austrian, Count de Koudenhove-Calergi, did not see the expression of their ideas of unification in these inter-governmental organisations. At the congress in The Hague in May 1948 a decision was taken that a political and economic union should be founded and that an Assembly should be called in order to discuss these plans. When exactly a year later the Council of Europe was founded its goals were rather more limited and its structure was still intergovernmental, but it did have an Assembly meeting in Strasbourg. The debate within the European Movement as to whether this assembly met The Hague Congress' intentions became quite heated. However, the question soon became irrelevant with the signing of the Treaty of Paris by six states eighteen months after Robert Schuman's famous declaration on 9 May 1950 proposing pooling of the essential resources of coal and steel. In the Treaty, the Common Assembly was actually invested with rather more power than some had feared and others hoped.

The Common Assembly had 78 members, all of whom also served in the Assembly of the Council of Europe. It met for the first time on 10 September 1952. Its first president, Paul Henri Spaak, could speak on equal terms to the governments of the member states as he had not only been prime minister himself, but had also been instrumental in drafting the Treaty of Paris. He was definitely a federalist, and his election can be seen as a precursor to the formation of transnational political groups, as socialists of all different nationalities were asked to vote for Spaak at the insistence of the French Socialist leader, Guy Mollet.

Another question to be settled was how to deal with the members of the Common Assembly not coming from one of the six signatory countries. The British Foreign Secretary Anthony Eden put forward a plan that the Assembly of the Council of Europe with all its members might serve as the Assembly for the ECSC as well. This plan to allow Britain to keep a finger in the pie was unacceptable to Monnet, although Eden announced that if his plan was not accepted Britain would have to reappraise its relations with the continent. Wellenstein by sheer coincidence met in the office of Max Kohnstamm with the US envoy to the OEEC and ECSC, Ambassador Bruce, who considered the British threat ludicrous. Monnet requested the legal advisors of the three big countries to give an opinion. On a report by Ophüls, de Rossi and Reuter it was decided that members from other countries might participate as observers with speaking rights, but not vote. In this same document most importantly it was decided that the rules of the Assembly were of an independent supranational nature, thus creating new law, not directed or dependent on rules of the national parliaments. Of the Eden plan nothing was subsequently heard, and the British and their parties have reappraised their opinion vis-à-vis the continent's integration plans on a number of occasions.

Although the Treaty of Paris had not met with much opposition in the parliaments of the member states, it was clear to all that this was only the first step towards further unification. It was typical, too, that the United Kingdom, which was a founding member of the Council of Europe, did not participate in the Coal and Steel Community and therefore not in the Common Assembly either. Historians have disagreed about the attitude that the British adopted at the Messina Conference, the initiative that led to the EEC Treaty. Interpretations range from sabotage to misjudgement. But given the fact that the debate in Britain as to whether to participate in further integrationist ventures, which were already being put forward in those days by visionaries such as Altiero Spinelli and Henk Brugmans, is still going on today, one might safely conclude that the process of European unification would never have come to where it is now if the United Kingdom had been a member from the beginning.

It must be conceded though that the launching of the EEC and Euratom treaties in 1957 met with considerably more opposition in the national parliaments than in the Common Assembly, where the first draft Treaty for Political Union had already been adopted four years earlier.

The members of the non-elected Parliament

From when the Treaty of Paris came into force in 1952 until the first direct elections in 1979 the members of the Assembly - the joint assembly for each of the three treaties from 1958 - were selected rather than elected. The composition of the national delegations generally reflected the composition of the parliaments of the member states, nomination by agreement of the leaders of the national parties rather than by even an in-house election. The situation was even more odd in the case of France and Italy as until the early seventies the communists who formed the second largest political force, were excluded. In this way a positive attitude towards integration was enhanced as important political forces opposed to the integration process were excluded.

This may not have had quite the beneficial effect expected, since working in the European Parliament served for many early and late opponents as an eye-opener. It was most clearly said by Barbara Castle when she left the Parliament: 'I was against Europe when I came here. I am no longer, even if I want a different Europe.' The German SPD, one of the most pro-integration forces nowadays was, like Labour, originally against the Treaty of Rome. Notable among German Social Democrat MEPs was Helmut Schmidt, who later as Chancellor, together with Valery Giscard d'Estaing, was an initiator of Monetary Union. His attitude, however, was not so much anti-integrationist as dictated by the harbour interests of his constituency, Hamburg, which feared that a continental customs union might harm their shipping lines with the UK and the USA. The same attitude was to be found also in Rotterdam, lead by the President of the Chamber of Commerce, the influential Liberal, Dr K.P. van der Mandele.

In general, however, the members who were selected were of two categories: those with a 'cast-iron' mandate, who could afford to be absent from the national scene, and the European idealists. An important exception to this was the Dutch Christian Democratic party, very much in favour of integration, which considered some European experience as a necessary qualification for its up-and-coming young hopefuls, including their first woman cabinet minister, Marga Klompé, and virtually all future ministers for the 1970s. But definitely not all parties looked on a tour of duty in Strasbourg in such a positive light.

In the early days the European Parliament was not by far such a time consuming institution as it is nowadays. I speak from my own experience as a member who took his mandate seriously and was away from home and constituency every single week from Monday to Friday. But even if the Common Assembly met only three times a year for ten days (travel was not as easy as it is today, and to get from faraway places like the Azores or Lapland to Strasbourg can even now take one and a half days) being away from the national parliament for over thirty days a year, when it is in session, would exclude any member from a serious role in the day-to-day national political forum. It should also be noted that press coverage of the European Parliament, more especially so in Strasbourg, has been notably less than in the national capitals, and that the means of communication in the 1950s were considerably less sophisticated and immediate than today. So members were really excluded from the national political scene. One could only afford that if either one had got the assurance of continuity from the party leadership or one had been serving one's constituency so well that there was no danger of being unseated.

It was this phenomenon that brought to the European Parliament many former French cabinet ministers of the Fourth Republic, Christian Democrat members from southern Italy, as well as Labour members from the old mould and with constituencies in areas where even a broomstick would have been elected so long as it wore a red rosette. This first category of impregnable members diminished with direct elections in 1979, but the Labour delegation was renewed root and branch more recently when Prime Minister Tony Blair changed the electoral system from the one member 'first past the post' to the list system in 1999. It was not without reason that for many years the joke in political circles in Germany went: 'Hast du noch ein Opa, schick ihm nach Europa' ('If you still have a granddad, send him to Europe'). The average age of members up to direct elections was considerably higher than afterwards. The reason for this might, however, not only be the fact that these oldies were difficult to unseat, but also that they were from the generation that experienced two wars during their lifetime and were therefore more motivated to strive for peaceful cooperation between the one-time belligerent nations.

A sub-category among the 'cast iron mandates' was made up of political leaders at national level. Among those who served, mostly for a short while in Strasbourg, were Willy Brandt, Jacques Chirac, Georges Marchais, Umberto Bossi and Enrico Berlinguer. If they came at all, they certainly did not participate in the day to day work and rarely in the debates in plenary.

If you were not in the first category of 'cast iron mandates,' you really had to be an enthusiast for European cooperation to volunteer for a mandate in the European Parliament, given the risk of not being re-elected. This happened to two of my former group, Presidents Cornelis Berkhouwer and Martin Bangemann, who were both sent as young freshmen from their national parliaments to Strasbourg and who both had great trouble in being re-elected for a second term. Many others did not have the same luck, skill and energy as these two, but their anonymous courage and devotion to the European cause is worth mentioning here.

One factor on which no research has been done is whether members are internationally inclined as a result of their family backgrounds. It is my unsubstantiated conviction that among my former colleagues many had different nationalities in their families, married foreigners or had lived abroad. This was their genetic or matrimonial motive for devotion to the European cause.

Some members could also be described as 'not in favour' with the party leadership and therefore best kept away in exile in Strasbourg. Unnecessary to say that they were rarely re-elected and anyway disappeared with direct elections, with the exception of diehard 'clause four' Labour members, some of whom held on until the fourth round of direct elections. An example of these members from my own party was Senator Jan Baas, who made his fame and senate seat by punching in public an extreme right former collaborationist colleague. This physical way of dealing in politics did not suit the sedate atmosphere of the Dutch Upper House and his group president considered it more appropriate for the company of southern European parliamentarians and therefore thought Strasbourg would maybe suit him well.

One of the consequences of the compulsory double mandate was that the 'choc des opinions' in Strasbourg had its effects at home. The European debate in the national parliaments was dominated by members of the European Parliament. This worked both ways insofar as the attitudes of the national parliaments were in return of consequence for the debates in the Strasbourg hemicycle. On top of that the national delegations were far smaller than later after direct elections, and met regularly both formally, assisted by the staff of the national parliaments who often doubled up as staff in the EP too, and also informally over dinner and drinks.

The informal atmosphere was influenced considerably by the temporary buildings that the Parliament rented from the Council of Europe in Strasbourg and from the Belgian government in Brussels. In Luxembourg the situation was a bit different. Only after 1973 was there a hemicycle there, offering the occasion for members to meet in Luxembourg at all, which they did six times a year until 1979. There were no private offices for the members in any of the three meeting places until the IPE building in Strasbourg was built at the initiative of Pierre Pflimlin, who happened not only to become President of the European Parliament from 1984 to 1987 but was also mayor of Strasbourg, a post he held for what seemed like a lifetime. He had also been the last prime Minister of the French Fourth Republic. Until the Palais de l'Europe was inaugurated in 1974, the Strasbourg meeting place was a temporary building not meant to last any longer than a few years. In this building there was only one common room, catering for everybody from chauffeurs and ushers to ministers and members. This created a tremendous sense of togetherness that was washed away the moment a class society was installed with dedicated bars and restaurants for different categories of users.

Apart from the bar 'Chez Yvonne' in the Parliament itself, each national delegation had its favourite hangout in town. For the Dutch it was each Tuesday evening at the 'Bourse au Vin.' When that closed one could always go to the station restaurant that remained open all night and was still adorned with one star in the Michelin guide. These evenings were mainly spent in heated discussion about national politics. It was here that the famous Den Uyl cabinet was formed by luring away a few Christian Democrat members of the EP from their party while the majority refused to negotiate with the Socialists.

Many members had an international background in one way or another and a knowledge of foreign languages, which made contact with other nationalities easier. Even if members were unable to speak foreign languages, the Parliament has facilities to encourage them to learn them, paying for courses and engaging permanent staff for language training. When I arrived in the Parliament, still composed of members from only six member states, French was the working language, spoken at all internal meetings, even if no French members were attending. More than half of the Liberal Group then consisted of French or French speaking members from Belgium and Luxembourg. With only one exception, Senator Armengaud, who represented the French living abroad in the Americas, none spoke any other language. But of the French in our Group in the 1989-94 legislature only one, a farmer from the département Haute Marne, did not speak English.

It was almost inevitable that once night sittings were introduced these informal get-togethers were doomed. And the sheer size of the delegations was even more of a hindrance to these meetings. It was already quite something to get a majority of the 14 Dutch members together, let alone when they became 25 after the introduction of elections and 31 since Maastricht. I personally have never seen all of them assembled in a single room. This would have been impossible for the larger member states - Germany now has 99 MEPs and the other three larger countries' 87 MEPs.

Political groups

Right from the start of the Common Assembly political allegiance played as much a role as nationality. At the constitutive meeting in September 1952 to elect a president members voted according to their party affiliation. Paul-Henri Spaak was elected by 38 votes to 30. Within a year an additional article was added to the rules, which allowed the formation of political groups. Possibly more instrumental was the funding for these on the basis of a fixed sum per group plus an additional amount per member. The minimum number required to form a group was nine (out of the total of 78) i.e.12%. Since then this rule has been adapted many times, most significantly to stimulate multi-nationalism, with the application of a differential according to the number of nationalities in a group. Only fourteen members are needed to form a political group (out of a total of 626) if the members are of four or more different nationalities. More are required if fewer nationalities are represented.

The first groups to be founded in 1953 were respectively the Liberals, the Christian Democrats and the Socialists. Even if named slightly differently, they still exist today. Later, many others were founded. In 1965, when the threshold to form a group was lowered, the Gaullists formed their own group, which grew in membership at successive enlargements of the Community with Irish, Greek and Portuguese parties. In the present Parliament it is now only the sixth largest.

In October 1973 the threshold was again lowered, this time to only ten (out of 198) members originating from at least three member states. This was done with the purpose of allowing the Communists, no longer blackballed by their national parliaments (mainly from Italy and France) to form their own group. Those members who would or could not adhere to a specific group formed a rag-tag grouping, the so-called Technical Group, later losing 'group status' to become simply independent or non-aligned members.

Quite another phenomenon is the merger between groups or, to put it another way, the swallowing of two smaller groups, the Conservatives and Forza Europa, by the currently largest grouping, the European Peoples Party (EPP), formerly the Christian Democratic group. Likewise the Italian Communists were taken into the Party of European Socialists.

After the accession of the United Kingdom and Denmark in 1973 a Conservative Group was founded, as mentioned above, which later joined the EPP in 1992; their Spanish allies in the Partido Popular having done so at the previous elections. Likewise the originally separate group of Forza Europa, the European arm of Silvio Berlusconi's Forza Italia, joined the EPP. This group emerged strongest from the 1999 elections and has been further strengthened by parties that previously had been in the Liberal group, such as the French UDF and the Portuguese PDS, both switching allegiance.

Other Groups formed were the Greens who together with some regional parties are now the fourth largest. During one session the Greens as a group joined with the short-lived right-wing Socialist grouping headed by Bernard Tapie. Personally I got along quite well with Tapie, especially as I had once, in my capacity as one of the three permanent rapporteurs on requests for waiver of parliamentary immunity, saved him from losing his immunity when the French Government wanted to start a court case against him for yet another soccer affair dating from five years earlier, but which they opened in order to prevent him from standing in the election for President of the Republic. I deemed this as political opportunism and a large majority of the House agreed with me.

There is still, notwithstanding the disappearance of the Communist regimes in Eastern Europe, a fundamentalist extreme left group, called Unified Left/Nordic Left.

Since the first enlargement an anti-integration force has been present within the Parliament. This Group comprised the Danish Anti-European Movement, the Dutch Calvinists, Ulster Unionists and now, in the recently elected Parliament, the French hunters and the UK Independence Party.

It has been typical of the European Parliament that over the years many individual members have changed groups. Smaller parties at the national political scene, not mustering enough votes, like Forza Italia, to form a group of their own in Strasbourg, were forced by the rules to seek alliances with other parties of different nationalities, with whom they often had very little in common. Otherwise, in a parliament that could not be dissolved, members who fell out with their party would demonstrate this break by sitting elsewhere until the end of their mandate. A few examples of this in the last legislature were the British Labour members Hugh Kerr and Ken Coates, who left their group for the Greens and the Communists respectively; the Christian Democrat Janssen van Raaij and the Socialist Van Bladel going to the Gaullists. None of them survived the subsequent elections. Those who change sides are seldom if ever re-elected, apart from the notable exception of the Luxembourg MEP, Astrid Lulling, who started her political career as a communist and has survived from the non-elected Parliament to the present day, where she now sits as an EPP member.

Powers

Even when the Parliament was only endowed with advisory powers, this did not necessarily mean that it had no influence. Just as in a non-political context, everything depends on the circumstances. Is the advice requested, and is the recipient receptive? Is the person who gives advice invested with enough authority?

The influence of the individual members in their national parliaments and in society at large has often been different to the influence of the parliament as an EU institution. For advice from the Parliament to be taken seriously by the Council and Commission, these institutions would have had to have been wanting and seeking advice; they usually weren't. This has mainly to do with the originally hybrid construction of the Community. Neither Council nor Commission were dependent for their nomination or survival on the Parliament. The Commission served more as a permanent sparring partner for the members, but to serve as a valid intermediary in the Council meetings it had to be trusted. Parliament had no access to Council-Commission meetings and where no minutes of the Council were published this indeed raised questions of trust.

Parliament had little opportunity to control the Council, despite the formal handing over of the Presidency every six months, where the incumbent promises a bright future and the outgoing President explains to Parliament that because of unforeseen and unlucky circumstances its promises could not be realised. At least the broken dreams were washed down with lavish dinners and quantities of champagne. A discussion between equals did not exist, as there was no balance in the decision-making powers. The situation improved after the Single European Act. Parliament was granted two readings of certain types of legislation and within limits enjoyed the power to propose amendments and a chance to see them enacted in Council legislation. Since the Maastricht Treaty the situation has changed fundamentally, as Council and Parliament are finally in direct contact and have to agree in order to get legislation realised at all. The role of the Commission in the final stages of the decision-making process has been reduced to that of an honest broker.

One might have expected that the Parliament, in its struggle for more power, would have used all the instruments at its disposal: Article 144, the motion of censure and Article 203, the budgetary procedure. Although this has been tried several times, they turned out to be sticks too big to handle.

The first time a motion of censure was filed was in the first year of my attachment to the Parliament as a staff member to the Liberal Group in 1972. The issue was a combination of both the budgetary rights and the political responsibility of the Commission vis-à-vis the Parliament. During the Dutch presidency of the Council in 1970 the EC was granted its 'own resources': a percentage of VAT, customs duties and agricultural levies. This dossier, too technical to be handled by the Foreign Secretary, Joseph Luns, was entrusted to my then employer, the junior minister for European Affairs, Hans de Koster. He insisted that with own resources the EC needed some accountability to an elected body; the Court of Auditors did not exist then. Thus it was agreed that the Commission would submit proposals on a procedure through which the Parliament could submit amendments on so-called 'non-obligatory expenditure' directly to the Council. After negotiations the final say on the proposal for the total budget proposals as returned from the Council would rest with the Parliament. When the Commission, having been requested to do so many times, had still not submitted these procedures by December 1972, the president of Parliament's budget committee, French senator Georges Spénale, then submitted a motion of censure. This would almost certainly have been adopted had not Commission President, Sicco Mansholt, who was to retire the following month having served on the Commission since 1958, made an emotional plea not to end his career this way. Thereupon, Spénale withdrew his proposal.

The Santer Commission stepped down in 1999 as a result of strong criticism from the Parliament, but a motion of censure has never yet been voted on and adopted. Although the responsibility of the Commission and its individual members towards Parliament has been settled, it is clear that over the years the institutional struggles of the Parliament shifted from the Commission to the Council. Initially the ground for confrontation was the budget and the procedure of Article 203, but with the co-decision procedure of the Treaties of Maastricht and Amsterdam it has been concentrated more on legislation. This is understandable as the bluntness and difficulty of the budgetary weapon might be illustrated by the rejection that directly followed the first direct elections in 1979 under the rapporteurship of Piet Dankert, who was later to become the President of the Parliament in succession to Simone Veil. This exercise backfired since the ministers of finance noticed with some glee that this rejection served them rather better than anybody else. If a budget is rejected, payments can only be made for adopted policies to the amount of one twelfth of the budget of the previous year, paid each month, until a new budget is submitted and adopted. Finance ministers saw this as a heaven-sent opportunity to save money.

Although the influence of the Parliament on the budget is not negligible - in the sense that some items are added or given more emphasis - it took until Maastricht to create other meeting grounds between Parliament and Council, and in that way it was more important symbolically than for its direct financial implications. On any other issue the Council could permit itself to ignore Parliament.

The extent to which this was indeed the case might be best explained in a slightly anecdotal way. In the early eighties a member of the Parliament became a minister in a national government. In her first Council meeting a disagreement between the member states arose, and in order to seek a compromise solution the minister asked the Council secretariat to inform the Council of the advice of the Parliament, which had already dealt with the question. The reply given by the Secretary General of the Council was that indeed the advice of the Parliament had been received. At this reply the minister, assuming the interpretation of her question had not been quite clear, repeated her request, in slightly simpler terms, seeking the content of the advice. It turned out nobody present in the Council meeting, including the Commissioner entrusted with this issue, had the slightest knowledge of the content of the advice given by Parliament. Nobody cared, as long as the formal requirement could be met that no decision be finalised until the Parliament had given its advice by a formal vote in the hemicycle.

In its attempts to find a solution to this situation of benign neglect a stroke of luck came Parliament's way at the very end of the non-elected period. During the summer recess of that year the Commission issued a new regulation on isoglucose, the converted sugar substitute made from wheat, potato or corn. This regulation had not received the opinion of the Parliament for lack of time as it figured as the very last item of the last session before elections. But rapporteur Tolman (EPP), who did not stand for re-election, let the issue drop when it was pointed out there was no quorum present in the Chamber. Some isoglucose firms - Roquette Frères from France and Maizena Gmbh from Germany - who all of a sudden got lower subsidies from agricultural funds, filed a request for annulment at the Court of Justice. The Parliament as an institution joined the plaintiffs. The Court ruled that indeed any legislation on which the Parliament had not given its advice was null and void.

At the initiative of the legal affairs committee, notably Sir Christopher Prout, the Parliament adapted its rules in such a way that from then on no final vote would be taken, unless the Commission committed itself to defending the viewpoint of Parliament in Council. This weapon, ingenious as it appeared, lost its edge rather soon as the Commission hid behind its collective responsibility, refusing to give a reaction once Parliament had voted. Later it would give as a rapid reply a long list of numbers of amendments it could or could not accept, making a bingo session seem slow by comparison. When the Council eventually took a decision, promises by the Commission had mostly been forgotten. Even if they had not, there were hardly any remedies other than sacking the whole Commission, which was out of the question as it was ultimately not the Commission but the Council which refused to adopt Parliament's viewpoint. For many years now this procedure has been reported in a written form, called 'suites données,' which is put on the agenda of each session, but virtually never gives sufficient reason to hold a real debate. It's more an administrative matter which can at least can be checked carefully by staff of each of the institutions, and by scholars for the records.

Exerting pressure on the Commission certainly brought Parliament more influence, but the Commission remained at best a messenger that could not be controlled, since the Council meetings were and still are held behind closed doors. When you look at the results, that is the ideas from Parliament which reach final texts in the Official Journal, the best you can say is that they are meagre. Still, some progress towards a truly controlling role was started with the isoglucose judgement, and as long as Council reproached the Commission for being too much on Parliament's side, (the Commission told the Council exactly the opposite), there was at least some balance.

The European Parliament all too often lost itself in too many detailed amendments on all kinds of technical legislation, points that in a national context would not even have been considered by Parliament at all, but dealt with in administrative procedures. In the EC what was lacking in depth was compensated for in width. Even now that the Parliament has got co-decision power with Council, this is still the case. The long hours of voting in the hemicycle on minute detail could be better used in more fundamental debate and exchange of arguments instead of holding short debates, where each intervention lasts on average less than three minutes, limiting the intervention to the bare essentials in order to make time for voting.

13/83 or failure to act

The second occasion when the Parliament extended its powers was again with the help of the Court of Justice. The President of the Transport Committee, the German SPD member Horst Seefeld, seconded again by the Legal Affairs Committee, succeeded in filing a complaint on behalf of the Parliament against the Council for non-implementation. Twenty-two proposals on transport matters had been submitted by the Commission and Parliament had given its opinion on them, but the Council had failed to reach agreement, and thus they remained unimplemented. In the Court, the Council defended itself with the argument that differences of opinion were such that they could not take a vote. The judgement given in May 1985 discarded this argument on the grounds that Article 75 of the Treaty prescribed that beyond the transition period, which finished in 1970, the Council had to decide by majority voting.

The coincidence of this judgement with the agreement on the Single European Act, which introduced the cooperation procedure, opened up borders for the liberalised internal market, and speeded up affairs considerably. It was unthinkable that internal borders would disappear, thus boosting internal trade by making goods circulate freely, without creating at the same time the practical means that goods might be transported from one member state to another.

At this time Parliament seemed to fall into the same trap as the Council, discussing endlessly whether harmonisation of conditions under which to allow transporters to cross borders (for which until then they needed a permit) had to come before liberalisation. Harmonisation turned out to be virtually impossible as this did not only apply to transport matters but to social conditions as well; drivers in one member state earned considerably more than in others and their social security situations were quite different.

The outcome of this process was not only that the Treaty and its obligations were to be taken more seriously, but that Parliament could also force the other institutions to pay more attention to its wishes. The recognition of the Parliament as an institution parallel to the Council and the Commission as mentioned in Article 175 was at the same time the recognition of a certain power of initiative.

Other court cases

From then Parliament was less successful when it turned to the Court in order to get its powers enhanced. With mounting work pressure on the Court, especially in competition cases, it tried not to be dragged in deeper in Parliament's search for more power. After an initial refusal in the Comitology affair, where the Court considered that the Parliament should resort to political rather than legal methods, a successful plea was introduced in the Chernobyl case where it declared that if the Parliament was not consulted again, after the Commission had introduced major changes to proposals at a later date, these proposals would be annulled. Later, however, the Court became more reticent and stated, in a new request for a declaration of non-implementation on the issue of installing EU-wide border controls at the external frontiers, that if political routes were open, legal action by Parliament was not a correct procedure. The case was declared non-receivable.

The Court's constitutional role has become one of distance or withdrawal, as is clearly shown in my own case. I provoked the judges to take a stance on the same question of the suppression of border controls (as written in Articles 7a and 8a of the Treaties), since I deemed it difficult as a candidate to confront the electorate with agreed policies that simply could be discarded or neglected by the member states. Apparently the Court is so submerged in the simple administration of the law that it can no longer be a guide on the path to the fulfilment of the goals of the Treaties. It might be that this role is now to a large extent being taken over by the specific national constitutional courts, where the transfer of sovereignty is challenged. This has been the case in Denmark, Ireland and most significantly at the Bundesverfassungsgericht in Karlsruhe, Germany. In its 'So Lange' judgement this court ruled that no more sovereignty should be transferred from the member states to the Union, unless democratic control was also transferred simultaneously.

From co-operation to co-decision

Every time the Treaties have been revised some democratic advance has been built in to satisfy the European Parliament. In the Single European Act of 1987 it was decided that anything necessary to establish the internal liberalised market was to be decided by simple majority in the Council as drafted in Article 100a of the Treaty. At the same time the Treaty announced that such a measure would need a second reading by the Parliament. Called the cooperation procedure it meant that amendments adopted in second reading with the absolute majority of members could only be overturned at the final stage by the Council acting unanimously. Because of widespread absenteeism and the political differences between groups it was not easy to muster the required number of votes in Parliament (313 after the last enlargement). Inevitably this led to compromises, mainly between the largest political groups, whilst in the Council it quickly led to informal agreements not to accept any changes to the difficult compromises reached between the member states at the first Council reading: the common position. The process in the Council of coming to a common position represents an anomaly among the different decision-making processes, since there is no time limit imposed. When there is a disagreement in the Council, proposals can drag from one Presidency to another until some form of compromise, often a joint effort by the Presidency and the Commission, is reached. As it tends to be so difficult to reach these compromises, the influence of the Parliament in later stages is minimised. Once it has reached its compromise, the Council agrees not to restart discussions in the light of Parliament's amendments. And yet, compared to the ineffectual consultation procedure which preceded it, from the Parliament's view the cooperation procedure was considered an improvement.

Once in a while the Parliament tried to change the legal basis of Commission proposals in order to shift its influence from mere advice to the cooperation procedure. In general the Court has not been very receptive to these attempts, although once in a while it did declare Council decisions null and void, in particular if they were too different from the original proposal on which the Parliament had given its initial opinion. You win some, you lose some.

The Council, pressed by either national courts or parliaments, felt enough pressure to adapt the decision-making process in favour of the Parliament twice in the last few years, in the Maastricht and Amsterdam Treaties. It remains to be seen if it will again do so at the IGC taking place in 2000. The largest step towards a fully-fledged co-legislative Parliament took place in the Treaty of Maastricht which introduced the co-decision procedure. It seems that each time that the integration process is taken a step further, the Heads of State and Government deem it necessary to concede something to the Parliament.

This process started as early as 1974, when the European Council (at that time still entitled 'Summit Conference'), under the chairmanship of French President Giscard d'Estaing, later to become my group leader, decided that the vicious circle of 'one can not elect a Parliament that has no powers, and a non-elected Parliament can't have real powers' should be broken. He needed a success for his Paris summit and the other eight participants could think of no reason to refuse. The President of the European Parliament,

Cornelis Berkhouwer, whom I then served as chef de cabinet, rushed to Paris to thank him personally, since he had been the one to suggest this move when he met Giscard before the summit. It was a first and major step, a sea-change in the nature of the Parliament. Nowadays, the Parliament's President is admitted at the opening of the European Council's meetings for a few minutes to deliver a speech outlining the wishes of Parliament. Those present in the European Council listen closely to that speech, ask a few questions and then allow the speaker to leave again while they get on with business. One might ask which method was more effective, Berkhouwer's informal conversations or the present procedure, and whether the present one, where the Parliament's President is asked to leave after the first hour or so, is not meant to be somewhat degrading.

Once the Parliament was elected, its quest for powers changed from behind the scenes influence and dominating the discussion on European issues in national parliaments to a much more overt powerplay on confrontational lines with other institutions. The recent crisis which forced the Commission to step down is an example of success for the Parliament. But one might ask if it is possible to come to a similar showdown vis-à-vis the Council. It is not through conciliation in the co-decision procedure, as the result of institutional disagreement can only be that there will be no legislation at all. Nor is it by means of the other weapons that the Parliament can exert on the Council. As shown above it is not the rejection of the budget, nor even the vetoing of enlargement, where the Parliament has to give its assent. The biggest flaw in the division of powers between the institutions remains the fact that the Parliament, contrary to national parliaments, is not required to ratify Treaty changes, although it has to apply and uphold the Treaty once it is changed.

The Parliament might use the eventual refusal to approve enlargement as a lever to get more powers, but that is both unfair to the applicants and in breach of the preamble of the Treaty. The last time the Union was enlarged the

Parliament did not have the courage to withstand the pressure exerted overtly and behind the scenes by the governments of the member states on the members. In my personal opinion that could have been a good occasion to strike a deal with the Council. The Parliament should have stated that it would only vote for enlargement if the Council committed itself to Parliament's wishes on institutional reform as formulated and voted on by the members. With only a few others I voted against in the first vote on Norway, but when I found out that only 23 other members were prepared to follow that course, I changed my vote, on Austria, Sweden and Finland, to abstention.

The fact that two representatives of the Parliament are admitted to the IGC preparatory committee is definitely no remedy to the lack of influence on Treaty changes. Last time, on the preparatory committee to Amsterdam under the chairmanship of the Dutch junior minister Michiel Patijn, the two representatives of the Parliament were Elisabeth Guigou (PES), now herself Minister of Justice in the French government, and Elmar Brok (EPP) a man in the confidence of former Chancellor Helmut Kohl. Whenever real negotiations in this preparatory group took place these two were requested to leave the room. On other occasions the real negotiations took place behind their backs. It remains to be seen whether things will be very much different in the 'leftovers IGC' that is taking place in 2000 under the French presidency. The jury is still out, but there is much less at stake for the Parliament, since it was well treated at Amsterdam despite being marginalised in the negotiations. The 2000 IGC concerns mainly voting in the Council and the composition of the Commission.

Looking at the development of Parliament's powers and the depth of its influence, I think we went far beyond what was anticipated in the early seventies, and even then we were considered unrealistic idealists. Parliament's powers have developed beyond the demands of the early federalists. The correspondence of the then President of the European Federalist Movement in the Netherlands, my colleague Hans Nord, who later became Secretary General of the European Parliament and was subsequently elected in the first direct elections, shows that he made a general plea for a constitution, but not even he ever mentioned a co-legislative directly elected assembly.

Parliament somewhat modestly calls on the Commission to make proposals in this IGC on Treaty changes, but it has put forward quite a few daring and pertinent requests itself in an impressively comprehensive document: first and foremost that Article 48 be reformed so that the Parliament has the right of assent to future Treaty changes, and that the Treaties be redrafted as one single text with two parts, a constitutional section and one containing sectoral policies as written down in the present treaties.

Legislation and members

Given the huge differences between the early years, when grand designs were discussed in Parliament, and the present day, where the Parliament has been transformed into a legislative machine producing thousands of amendments every month on the most intricate and detailed directives and regulations concerning everyday household problems, such as consumer protection for products bought in direct sales or the noise levels of motorised lawn-mowers, one might ask whether the influence of the Parliament has really increased. Would not a return to a somewhat more aloof stance, discussing such issues as Common Defence and Security Policy, not attract more attention from the media and the electorate at large?

One might even wonder if it has not been a deliberate policy by the members of the European Council to involve the Parliament more in the detail of everyday legislative work, instead of having it looking over their shoulder when they discuss important issues such as EMU, further enlargement and foreign policy, the pooling of military resources and intervention in the Balkans. Paul Henri Spaak, whilst still President of the Parliament, once said to a journalist: 'Now that we have started a debate on a levy of 0.25% on cocoa, the Parliament is finished.' What Parliament lacked from the beginning in influence on the real course of the integration process has been obscured in many ways by the width of the issues covered by the co-decision and cooperation procedures on minute pieces of legislation. In many a national parliament these would not even have figured on the agenda of a committee meeting, but would simply have been communicated to members under administrative rules and procedures. What use is it to a real integration of the peoples of Europe that the Parliament has had its say on many amendments adopted on the step-heights of agricultural machinery or the digitalisation of control instruments in lorries, if on the issues of participation of soldiers of different nationalities in peacekeeping operations the one Parliament that represents the European electorate at large has nothing influential to say? Even if it has an opinion on such issues, the Council which takes these decisions does not have to pay any attention and can do so without any fear of political sanctions from Parliament.

Partly this is due to the organisation of work and debates in Parliament itself, and is not to be seen as a matter of inter-institutional dispute. In the non-elected period members were too occupied keeping their feet on the ground in two parliaments at once to have time and energy to spare on details.

The group secretariats, even if the groups were less than a tenth in size of what they are today, played a much larger role, deciding between them which issues would be discussed and who would be a rapporteur. There were so few members who knew anything about specific technical subjects that fighting between groups about which one of them would deal with a specific issue was out of the question.

Today there are so many members who each have to explain and defend to their constituents what a useful job they are doing that in the division of rapporteurships many are eager to take responsibility even for the minutest piece of legislation. Since direct elections these have been taken on by members themselves and therewith politicised, instead of agreed upon by staff on the grounds of competence. Members want to see experts and lobbyists and prepare a good number of mainly technical amendments. All this in the vain hope of attracting the attention of the press. That rather the opposite is the case has up to now not led to a substantial change in procedure.

A few attempts have been made, nonetheless. One was to create Article 55 of the rules of procedure, which allows committees to decide on technical matters which are then no longer discussed in plenary. Up to now this has been rarely used, mainly because technical matters often get rapporteurs either from the smaller groups or those members that do not often get the occasion to file a report. They often insist on discussion in plenary. A second flaw to the application of this article is the fact that the composition of committees is not always strictly balanced. The Environment Committee, for example, attracts members who do not necessarily represent the same balance as Parliament as a whole but are more open to environmentalists' arguments. The mirror image of the Environment Committee is represented by the Economic and Monetary Affairs Committee, which is more inclined to reflect the ideas of the industrial and business sector.

Another difficulty in livening up parliamentary procedure is multilingualism. In itself it is understandable that a multinational, multicultural parliament allows its members each to express themselves in their mother tongue. But this makes it impossible to allow interruptions, since it would hold up proceedings too much if, for example, a Greek speaker, being interrupted in Finnish, would have to stop his speech to listen to the interpretation, and vice versa for the member interrupting him.

Still, this is not the only reason why there is relatively seldom an interesting debate in the hemicycle. The recent introduction of the 'free-for-all' debate with the Commission is definitely an improvement. But the regular debates remain boring, mainly since the introduction of the limited speaking time, which can limit a member to as little as one minute. This not only restricts speakers to the bare essentials, which then necessarily become repetitive; it also allows the Commission or the Council too easily to limit their answers and reactions to the prepared technical speeches of their civil servants. As there is no second round of debate, they can get away with these generalities without the possibility of contestation. Parliamentary control is emasculated.

The dreariest of all are the endless voting sessions, which to all but a few members, such as rapporteurs and the spokespeople for the groups, are an incomprehensible list of numbers on which groups, on the indication of their whips, vote for, against or abstain. Since the text that is being voted on is not visible to the public or the press, this is an incomprehensible spectacle. It is not that the amendments are not available, although often only a few minutes before the votes, but the number is such that it is on occasion well nigh impossible to physically carry to one's seat hundreds of amendments. Even if one could, the speed and the order of the voting is such that it is still impossible to read the text, vote and rationally assess the impact of the outcome of the votes all within seconds.

I often proposed in the Rules Committee, of which I was President for a while and a very active member during the full period of my mandate, that Parliament should reduce these long hours by voting only on amendments that contest a majority vote in the competent committee. Indeed, this used to be the case before the introduction of the cooperation procedure. The argument against change has been that for a co-legislative institution, any amendment to the proposed text originally proposed by the Commission should be voted on separately in plenary. I don't see why the uncontested opinion of a parliamentary committee could not be assumed to be the view of the majority of members of Parliament. After all, any group or 29 members can always submit new amendments to the plenary, independently of their participation in committee procedure, as indeed often happens.

A final reason why the debates in Parliament do not attract much attention from the media is the relative isolation of Strasbourg. European journalists based in Brussels have few reasons to travel there as long as news is also made at the same time in Brussels. If necessary they can ask for and get all the information they want in Brussels from the press services of the Parliament and its political groups; phone, fax, e-mail, internet and TV give them ample reason to stay away.

The seat

Siting the original Coal and Steel Community in Luxembourg was almost an accident. Many places were under consideration. Brussels, or at least Belgium, was already among the locations under consideration and quite acceptable to the representatives of the six member states. However, the Belgians, with their eternal language and other cultural divisions proposed Liège, but Prime Minister Van Zeeland would not upset that national linguistic compromise. The French government was considering Saarbrücken, capital of the Saarland, part of Germany, in the very heart of the coal and steel producing areas, and at that moment still under French administration, and a possible symbol of new Franco-German relations. Saarbrücken, however, was still heavily damaged as a result of wartime allied bombing and much of its population was still temporarily housed. It would have been untenable to build new lodgings for the High Authority and its staff without having adequate housing for the ordinary people. The Italians offered Turin, which was about to be adopted, when Adenauer, who had been dozing in the meeting, woke up and vetoed it.

In the Council it was the Luxembourg Prime Minister, Joseph Bech, who offered to accommodate the ECSC temporarily in a empty building of the Railway Company (CFL) at the station side of the Pont Adolphe bridging the Alzette in Luxembourg. Since Luxembourg was no threatening influence on the institutions, was situated in the coal and steel producing heartland, had been incorporated in the German Reich during the war, and incidentally was the birthplace of Robert Schuman, this offer was graciously accepted by all six governments, and the CFL staff were evicted overnight. When the three executives were merged some years later the building was taken over by the European Investment Bank.

For the Common Assembly, however, there was no suitable meeting room available in the Grand Duchy. Its own small parliament of just fifty members was housed in an outbuilding of the Grand Duke's palace and did not use interpretation facilities. Since the members of the Assembly doubled as members of the Parliamentary Assembly of the Council of Europe in Strasbourg they continued meeting there. The buildings were temporary, meant to be replaced within two years, but lasted until the Palais de l'Europe was inaugurated sixteen years later in 1974.

In 1958 when the ECSC was extended with the Treaty of Rome and Euratom, the intention was to install the new institutions in Luxemburg, too. This, however, met with the opposition of the Luxembourg clergy, who looked with suspicion on the prospect of all the strangers about to mix with their very traditional and faithful flock. The Bishop, having had enough foreign experience with the ECSC staff in previous years, intervened and conferred with the Grand Duchess Charlotte, who in turn let the Luxembourg government know this view. They decided not to offer to host the new institutions. Had they ignored this advice, Luxembourg would now perhaps be the D.C. of Europe. Instead, the new EEC and Euratom Commissions, on the explicit wish of EEC Commission President Walter Hallstein, moved to the nearest capital which was not of the larger member states, being both accessible and still, like Luxembourg or the Saarland, on the borderline of two cultures. Brussels was the choice.

From then onwards the European Parliament, of which membership now became separated from the Council of Europe's Assembly, started to hold committee meetings in the same place where the Commission and its staff, who were required to attend those meetings, were settled. The first of those meetings was held in the Belgian Senate, which, because of Belgium's trilingualism, also disposed of interpretation facilities. Later they were transferred to semi-permanent facilities at the Congress Centre at the Coudenberg, and later still to their own parliamentary premises on the Rue Belliard, most recently moving into the luxurious development of new buildings for the European Parliament nearby.

It took quite a while before the plenary sessions in Strasbourg came under any criticism at all. A year after British, Danish and Irish entry in 1973 a new building and hemicycle was opened in Luxembourg, where the Parliament was due to meet six times a year. The Council had already been meeting in Luxembourg for three months each year. When after direct elections the Parliament was enlarged, the Parliamentary Hall in the Schuman building in Luxembourg proved too small, but it took the Luxembourg government too long before they decided after many quarrels to construct a new hemicycle in Luxembourg at the Kirchberg, adjoining the Council meeting rooms. Strasbourg stepped into the breach. The Parliament has only met twice in the Luxembourg hemicycle. It lacked adequate facilities for members and once the IPE I building in Strasbourg with private offices for each of the members had been finished, Parliament never returned to Luxembourg, leaving there only a hard core of about 1000 support staff and administrative services. However, according to the decisions taken in accordance with Article 216, by which the governments of the member states decide in common agreement about the seat of institutions, the Council still meets three months a year in Luxembourg - April, June, October - when the city and countryside look their best.

The IPE I building was the start of an extensive building programme and the efforts by the Strasbourg administration and the French government to do everything possible to keep the Parliament in the city, although it was becoming rather reluctant to continue its vagrant existence. It is, however, not true that the bathrooms in the IPE I members' offices were added for this purpose. This was done at the insistence of the financiers of the IPE project, the Dutch building industry pension fund, who wanted to be able eventually to convert the building into a student or congress hostel, if pressures in the Parliament to abandon Strasbourg in favour of Brussels finally led one day to Parliament moving.

Once the European Council in Edinburgh, at French insistence and with British agreement, had taken a definite decision on the seat of the institutions, several other buildings were added to the Strasbourg complex, culminating in the new hemicycle and members' offices in the Louise Weiss Building, which opened in July 1999.

In Brussels, however, there was an equal rush of building activity. The Parliament was temporarily lodged in a rather decrepit building near the Central Station at the Boulevard de l'Empereur, with only three permanent meeting rooms and a few offices for the secretariats of the political groups. That lasted from 1976 to 1979, and Parliament had to organise some extra committee space in the Belgian Government's Palais d'Egmont. It gradually moved to the European Quarter around Rondpoint Schuman, and to Rue Belliard with two building complexes and a visitor centre in the nearby Eastman Building in Parc Leopold. Finally it moved to magnificent new premises on the Rue Wiertz. The Rue Wiertz building, popularly entitled 'Caprice des Dieux,' because its main building resembles a cheese of that name, was originally a private initiative inspired by Banque Générale CEO and former Commissioner Viscount Etienne Davignon and the Blaton

Building Enterprise. As if by accident, it was tailor made to the wishes of the European Parliament, and included a large enough hemicycle to match the Parliament's growing membership. When an additional building with committee rooms and members' private offices, called the Spinelli building after the federalist Altiero Spinelli, was added to the hemicycle building, Brussels was confirmed de facto as the day-to-day working place. Nevertheless this was not accepted without some legal struggle and some scandal.

At the request of the French government the Court of Justice condemned the Parliament and compelled it not to reduce its number of sessions in Strasbourg below twelve a year, except in election years, when only eleven would be required. The scandal erupted when, during the construction of the Spinelli building, bathrooms originally not foreseen had to be added to the members offices at the cost of $14,000 each. Personally, although not really in need of a bathroom with showers (my apartment in Brussels was just five minutes walk away) I made good use of the space as I stored my bicycle in it. This put me at loggerheads with the College of Quaestors, who are in charge of internal administrative arrangements affecting MEPs. I deemed this College useless anyway and would frequently write them letters about nonsensical subjects in order to keep them out of other mischief. This time it was specifically the Labour member, Richard Balfe, who considered my cycling in the buildings 'against safety, security and dignity.' It didn't take me much reflection to leak this correspondence to the press. The British tabloids in particular made quite something out of it, describing him as a *'stuffed shirt,'* who had forgotten how the miners used to keep their coal in the bath.

It is regrettable that at considerable cost to the taxpayer such architectural monstrosities both in Strasbourg and Brussels had to be built. Fixing one seat for the Parliament, was sadly as much a question of coincidences as one of national prestige, and the saga is not finished yet.

Relations with national parliaments

When there was a double-mandate for all MEPs in the non-elected Parliament, relations with the national parliaments were not an issue. Discussions about European policies in the national parliaments until 1979 were more or less necessarily lead by the EP members. Henk Vredeling, a former MEP and former Commissioner, told me once that they knew so much more about what was going on in the Community that they even had to inform national ministers and their civil servants about the latest developments in Brussels.

After direct elections this has become a difficult and in some countries strained relationship. National administrations, mainly via the working groups of the Council, which are staffed by the permanent representations in Brussels, are much better informed and often do not want to communicate that knowledge to the national parliaments. Otherwise ministers and civil servants might be hampered in their freedom to negotiate. One example of the will of the national parliamentarians to keep control over these processes is the Danish parliament, which through its Common Market Committee has kept tight control over the room for manoeuvre of the representatives of their country in the Council. This has annoyed some of the ministers so much that the foreign minister, Uffe Elleman Jensen, insisted during one of the more difficult negotiations over the Maastricht Treaty on calling the members of the national parliament's EU committee every other hour for a full night, just to show them what such close control could mean for them in lost sleep. The vehement protests of the sleepless committee members about this gave him the room he wanted for negotiations later on.

Some other parliaments have tried to copy the Danish model, but this example itself is no longer working as it used to. It apparently is not so easy now to follow day-to-day European affairs from the national capitals. Oddly enough, this goes even for those who have their seats at the very heart of European politicking, Brussels and Luxembourg. The Bundestag has had a tremendous boost in its capacity to sanction and control the national government after the 'So Lange' judgement of the German Constitutional Court but national parliaments seem in general incapable on their own to effectively exert power over their executives as far as European matters are concerned.

On one occasion the European Parliament, which is required to give its assent on trade agreements with third countries, was at a certain moment short circuited and tried to recoup via their national colleagues. The Commission had made a proposal on a Trade Agreement with Romania, then still under the yoke of Ceausescu's successor and former crony Iliescu, who violently tried to curb student protests by calling out the loyal miners. The European Parliament was in session and got rightly upset about this, asking the Commission to postpone the adoption of this agreement. Commissioner Bruce Millan, himself an ex-trade unionist, representing the Commission at that moment, agreed. The astonishment and even anger in the Parliament was great when a fortnight later the Council nonetheless approved the trade agreement with Romania. A request was sent out immediately to all national parliaments to question their governments about this. The reply turned out to be revealing. In five national parliaments the governments declared that they were against as well, but could not on their own resist the wish of eleven other member states. Mutual information was not speedy and accurate enough for the national parliaments to contradict this misrepresentation.

Another method was used in the run-up to the Maastricht Treaty. The European Parliament convened delegations from all national parliaments to a joint conference in Rome in order to agree on minimum conditions that all parliaments would insist on in the ratification procedure. When the acting Council President, Dutch Prime Minister Ruud Lubbers, came to debate the results in Strasbourg and the proposed Treaty did not fulfil the minimum standards agreed in Rome, his reply to the questions of the members as to how this could have been possible was 'Nobody in the European Council referred to the Rome conclusions of their national parliaments,' but indeed all approved the results. The conclusion is that no majority in a national parliament would risk voting against its government, provoking its fall and new elections, since this might mean losing its domestic majority over all European issues.

From then onwards the European Parliament understood that it had to act on its own and fight for its own ratification and co-legislative powers, since it could not count on the support of national parliaments. Indeed one might say that relations have not improved since and that direct contact between EP members and their national counterparts, even within the same parties, are always under strain. With the growing percentage of secondary law, this is regrettable since both the European and national parliaments represent the same electorate. It could be considered a waste when they deal with the same issues over which, in more and more cases, through co-decision after conciliation meetings, a compromise has been found directly between the EP and the Council. The text could easily be explained and even improved if the members of the EP were given the possibility to join in with their national colleagues when they deal with those same issues in their national parliaments. The MEPs are better informed and do not have to redo all the work. Here lies an important task for the European and national presidencies in their twice yearly meetings: to come to better future parliamentary cooperation instead of competition and, sometimes, conflict.

Conclusions

As I write, a new IGC is taking place, where fundamental choices are to be made as to whether the EU is to be a real federation of European nations or an organisation of national states with several joint policies, just allowing some deeper forms of cooperation between some of the member states. It is important to establish what the role of the Parliament was meant to be and what it will be.

It was in The Hague, my home town, immediately after the second world war, that Winston Churchill and the Congress of The Hague issued their clarion call to European politicians. For a long while the European Parliament was an assembly of national politicians, who on the basis of idealism and the will to avoid new conflicts between the nations of Europe, got together to discuss among themselves and with their national leaders ways and means to reach these goals. Mistrust of Germany and the search for ways to embed this nation in joint policies and procedures were foremost in their minds. The ECSC was considered a useful method to do this as it intended to keep a close check on the production of the basic materials for heavy and war industry.

Very soon the aggressive imposition of Communist dictatorial rule on the countries of central and eastern Europe forced the ECSC member states to pool efforts both economically and militarily to keep their nations from undergoing the same fate.

Two countries, the United Kingdom and France, considered it their role and status not to engage in processes that would curb their sovereignty or their chances of remaining leaders at world level. They did not wish to be hampered in unilateral moves by their former enemy or some smaller countries. The United Kingdom did so by not participating in any venture in a supranational direction, whilst France, lead by General de Gaulle, did so by voting against European Defence Cooperation (EDC) in 1954, applying the policy of the empty chair in the sixties, and pulling out of NATO. Both steered the European Community in a more intergovernmental direction. That policy was bolstered by the entry of the United Kingdom and Denmark, whilst Ireland, the third new entrant in 1973, saw its membership more as means to escape from economic dependency on its former oppressor.

These developments led integration policy to concentrate on the nitty-gritty work of harmonisation of economic policies, with emphasis on the agricultural policies, as stated in the Treaty - to increase production, to ensure a fair standard of living for the agricultural community and fair prices for consumers. In the early post-war years 30% of employment was still in agriculture; nowadays it is barely 5%. Initially, over three quarters of the budget was spent on the Common Agricultural Policy (CAP); now less than half. The agricultural committee in the Parliament was composed of specialists, who did not easily accept interference by others in their affairs and who formed among themselves, together with employers and employees and the farming organisations united in COPA, an early model of consensus economics. In our Liberal Group alone we had five former ministers of agriculture. Each year in spring on the occasion of price-setting for the forthcoming season they would hold a separate meeting among themselves and afterwards announce to the other members that they had settled for a price rise between, say, 11% and 13%. Those who would politely and surreptitiously ask if they did not consider this a bit much, received the answer that if they ever wanted to be re-elected, they had better keep quiet. Even special currency rates were applied for internal trade and export subsidies of agricultural products, so that the benefits were not lost because of unforeseen currency fluctuations.

It was the Single Act and the liberalisation of the internal market that marked the transition from the predominance of agriculture to industry, to the trade and service orientation of the Community. The United Kingdom had restructured its agriculture earlier than any other member state and had been more industry and trade oriented from the nineteenth century onwards, and it was the Briton - originally anti-European, Conservative Commissioner Lord Cockfield - who lead this process. The single market marked both the start of new policies, and a change in the role of the Parliament. With the tremendous legislative programme to undo internal barriers and enhanced powers in the new cooperation procedure, the members became more administrators than politicians. They no longer led the way in philosophical and far-sighted initiatives like the ones inspired by former Commissioner Altiero Spinelli and his 'Crocodile Group' named after a famous restaurant awarded several stars in Michelin. Spinelli and his friends were the last survivors of the early federalist movement. When he was interned as an opponent of the Mussolini regime, all he got to read as political literature was an English publication entitled 'Federal Union,' considered harmless by his captors, but evidently of immense influence for subsequent historical developments.

The unsurpassed legislative programme of almost 300 directives and regulations that had to be dealt with by Parliament under the new cooperation procedure to establish this internal market changed the character of Parliament from an idealist debating society into a legislative machine. Nowadays some members are taking a new interest in the reform of the institutional framework, as it has to reviewed by the IGC for 2000 in the light of the next enlargement to the countries of central and eastern Europe. But the grand design of a federal state is not at the forefront of the minds of many members of the European Parliament.

If one reads the optimistic predictions in other publications by the Federal Trust and other publishers one might be possibly less pessimistic about the federal future. One MEP with a formidable theoretical knowledge about institutional affairs and with several academic publications about the Parliament to his name, Richard Corbett, has been an active member of the former Institutional Affairs and Rules Committees. He writes: 'While not all of its members have subscribed to the end-product of a federation, the parliament as a whole has played an important part in promoting the process of integration in that direction.' He confirms what I have been trying to explain at the beginning of this piece, that the members of the European Parliament 'acted as essential go-betweens in explaining the Community and its potential to national parties and in bringing national parties further into European discussions.' ('The European parliament and the idea of European representative government,' in John Pinder (ed.) *Foundations of Democracy in the European Union*, McMillan Press, 1999)

One commentator, David Coombes, writes 'MEPs themselves appear to be frustrated: despite the growth of the formal competences of the Parliament over the years, their status is questionable and the reputation of their institution uncertain.' (*Seven Theorems in Search of the European Parliament*, Federal Trust, 1999) He confirms my view that over the years the political majority in the Parliament will also designate a more politicised Commission that will no longer serve simply as an expression of the composition of the governments in the member states. Thus Parliament in this century could become an instrument of social change.

Another, Andreas Maurer, *(What next for the European Parliament*, Federal Trust, 1999) indicates the ever growing influence of the Parliament on directly binding legislation. He rightly points out as well that the instrument of parliamentary enquiries, though used only a few times, might turn out to be ultimately the most effective method of establishing an influence that will have a wider impact on the electorate at large as well as on administrators in the member states.

However, he indicates, too, that the institutionalised role of Council and Parliament, forced to come to compromises in conciliation, diminishes their political visibility, This is only partly to be compensated for by a more outspoken view of the rapporteurs. On this last point I slightly disagree with him for I think, the role of the rapporteur is to be seen more as an expert on behalf of the institution at large. Political implications and opinions should be expressed in a more pronounced manner by the spokespersons of the political groups.

Given the development of a new and separate class of politicians within the European Parliament, it is odd that they still have a tendency to see themselves both as representing European viewpoints back home and representing the interest of their national or regional constituencies in the European context. In this process the original, supranational or federal goals have become less visible. They should keep those ideas well in the forefront of their minds.

European integration has proved itself successful not only as the main method to avoid conflicts between people and nations in this part of the world, but the European Union will continue to realise the common goals as worded in the preamble to the Treaty: ensure economic and social progress, eliminate the barriers which divide Europe and improve the living and working conditions of the people. Members of the European Parliament in which I have had the privilege of serving for fifteen years are more than anybody else called on to express, embody and realise these goals.

Notes on the authors

Lord Plumb

President of the National Farmers Union from 1970, Henry Plumb was elected as a Conservative MEP in 1979. He led the European Democratic Group from 1982 to 1987 when he became the first (and to date only) Briton to be elected President of the European Parliament. Made a life peer in that year, he went on to become Co-President of the EU-ACP Joint Assembly from 1994 until he left Parliament in 1999. Currently he is Chairman of the International Policy Council for Agriculture, Food and Trade.

Carole Tongue

A Robert Schuman scholar and subsequently on the staff of the European Parliament, Carole Tongue was first elected as an MEP in 1984. She became Deputy leader of the European Parliamentary Labour Party in 1989. She is a Board member of the Westminster Foundation for Democracy and the Quaker Council for European Affairs. She left Parliament in 1999 and is now a senior consultant with ACE Associates in London.

Florus Wijsenbeek

Head of the private office of Cornelius Berkhouwer as President of the European Parliament, and also Secretary General of the Federation of European Liberals, Florus Weijsenbeek was elected as an MEP in 1984. He is a lawyer and former member of the European Commission legal service.

The Federal Trust's recent publications

'Can Europe Pay for its Pensions?' by **Dick Taverne**
(ISBN 0-901573-98-1/£11.95)

'Britain and Euroland', ten essays edited by **Stephen Haseler**
and **Jacques Reland** (ISBN 0-901573-07-8/£14.99)

'The Asian Crisis and Europe's Global Responsibilities'
by **Dr Yao-Su Hu** (ISBN 0-901573-92-2/£9.95)

'What Next for the European Parliament?' by **Andreas Maurer**
(ISBN 0-901573-90-6/£9.99)

'Seven Theorems in Search of the European Parliament' by **David
Coombes** (ISBN 0-901573-70-1/£9.99)

'Altiero Spinelli and the British Federalists' edited and introduced
by **John Pinder** (ISBN 0-901573-58-2/£17.95)

'Venture Capital in Europe' by **Harry Cowie**
(ISBN 0-901573-86-8/£12.95)

'Paying for an Enlarged European Union' by **Charles Jenkins**
(ISBN 0-901573-88-4/£10.00)

'A New Transatlantic Partnership' by **Geoffrey Denton**
(ISBN 0-901573-87-6/£9.95)

Forthcoming publications

'The EU and Kaliningrad: The consequences of EU enlargement
on Kaliningrad' edited by **James Baxendale, Stephen Dewar** and
David Gowan (ISBN 0-901573-18-3/£18.95)

'Choice and Representation in the European Union' edited by
Michael Steed (ISBN 0-901573-73-6/£9.99)

'A Charter of Fundamental Rights' **Federal Trust's Constitution
for Europe Series** (ISBN 1-903403-04-9/£16.95)

The Federal Trust's European Essays series

'The European Elections in Britain' **Agnes Batory**
£5 ISBN 1-903403-19-7

'Our Europe' **Jacques Chirac**
£5 ISBN 1-903403-17-0

'From Confederation to Federation' **Joschka Fischer**
£5 ISBN 0-901573-19-1

'One Currency - One Country?' **Christopher Johnson**
£5 ISBN 0-901573-17-5

'Telecoms: Liberalisation without Harmonisation?' **Iain Osborne**
£5 ISBN 0-901573-08-6

'How to Pay for Europe?' **Iain Begg**
£5 ISBN 0-901573-09-4

'Is Civil Society heard in Brussels?' **Adrian Taylor**
£5 ISBN 0-901573-06-X

'Steps Towards a Federal Parliament' **John Pinder** and
'The EP and Institutional Reform' **John Bruton**
£5 ISBN 0-901573-97-3

'European Ideas - Hungarian Realities' **István Hegedûs**
£5 ISBN 0-901573-93-0

Forthcoming essays

'Rebuilding Ethics in Eastern Europe' by **Martin Stransky**

'New Balance between the Institutions' by **Mark Gray**

"Pan-European Political Parties' by **Thomas Jansen**

Visit our website for all the latest information
www.fedtrust.co.uk